# Down to Earth

# Adobe Architecture: an old idea, a new future

# Down to Earth

Based on an exhibition at the Centre Georges Pompidou,
conceived and directed by Jean Dethier

Translated from the French by Ruth Eaton

*With 303 illustrations, 65 in color*

**Facts On File, Inc.**
460 Park Avenue South
New York, New York 10016

Based on the exhibition *Des Architectures de Terre*, conceived and directed by Jean Dethier and produced by the Centre Georges Pompidou, Paris, in collaboration with the Deutsches Architektur Museum, Frankfurt. First shown in Paris (October 28 1981 to February 1 1982), the exhibition subsequently went on tour to various museums in Europe, North America, and the Third World.

First published in France in 1981 as *Des Architectures de Terre* by the Centre Georges Pompidou, Paris.

© 1981 Centre national d'art et de culture Georges Pompidou, Centre de Création Industrielle, Paris
English edition © 1982 Thames and Hudson Ltd, London

First published in the USA in 1983 by Facts on File Inc. 460 Park Avenue South, New York, New York 10016

**Library of Congress Cataloging in Publication Data**

Dethier, Jean.
  Down to earth.

  1. Building, Adobe.    I. Title.
TH4818.A3D47  1983    693´.22     82-7270
ISBN 0-87196-691-3            AACR2
ISBN 0-87196-800-2 (pbk.)

Printed and bound in Spain.
D.L. TO: 788-1982

# Contents

# Foreword

Earth has been the most essential of building materials since the dawn of man. Nature set the example: termites built towers above ground and developed air circulation which prefigured modern ventilation processes; the 'potter' wasp and its cousin the 'mud-mixer' wasp used their mandible to knead and model vaults that were perfectly rounded, as if designed by architects.

From the earliest times man followed this example. He built dwellings, be they humble or elaborate, with materials that were closest at hand: out of fibres, leaves, stone or unbaked – 'sun-dried' – earth. Know-how was acquired and passed down. But, with the onset of the industrial revolution, bricks of baked clay and mass-produced materials such as cement, steel and glass gradually supplanted the basic elements of traditional construction. The development of transportation made it possible to bring building materials from far away; while the use of modern components and specialized construction techniques brought about the loss of craftsmanship and art that had given each locale its sense of place. As the technical as well as the cultural roots of traditional architecture began to die out, the very shapes of buildings were transformed.

But this trend cannot disguise the fact that unbaked earth is still the most viable building material for one-third of the world's population – predominantly the poor who remain on the sidelines of a money-economy that depends on manufactured materials. Furthermore, building with earth has become an important factor in planning new development. Following the recent energy crises, technological progress has been made in certain countries, and the enthusiasm of architects and land developers has aided in the spread of these new techniques. Today we are able to choose between conventional 'international architecture' and a more 'down to earth' approach that combines reasonable cost with traditional cultural motifs in a modern way. But only people who live with the problem of housing can make this choice, because they are the only ones who can create their way of life and decide how to project it through architecture. The day is coming when architecture will be for living, and not merely a spectator sport.

*Jacques Mullender*
*Formerly Director*
*Centre de Création Industrielle*

Ever since mankind first congregated in villages almost 10,000 years ago, unbaked earth has been one of the principal building materials used in every continent. Over one-third of the world's population still lives in earth houses today. In ancient times, unbaked earth was widely used in Mesopotamia and Egypt, while later on, Romans and then Muslims built in earth in Europe, Africa and the Middle East – as did the peoples of the Indus civilizations, Buddhist monks and Chinese emperors. During the Middle Ages, construction in unbaked earth was practised not only in Europe, but in North America by the Indians, in Mexico by the Toltecs and the Aztecs, and in the Andes by the Mochica. The Spanish conquerors of America took with them European techniques of earth architecture and grafted them onto traditions already established there. In Africa, this art was mastered in cultures as diverse as those of the Berbers, the Dogons, the Ashanti, the Bamilikes or the Haoussas, in the kingdoms of Ife and Dahomey and in the empires of Ghana and Mali.

Throughout the world, archaeological remains survive of cities built entirely of raw earth: history's earliest city, Jericho, begun almost 10,000 years ago; Çatal Hüyük in Turkey; Harappa and Mohenjo-Daro in Pakistan; Akhlet-Aton in Egypt; Chan-Chan in Peru; Babylon in Iraq; Zuheros near Cordoba in Spain; and Khirokitia in Cyprus. Very often, modern cities have been established on the sites of these ancient towns, and many recent buildings are also constructed out of raw earth. Examples of this include 'Lugdunum', the capital of Roman Gaul which later became the city of Lyons, and many of the cities born out of the Spanish conquest of the Americas, such as Santa Fe, the capital of New Mexico, and Bogotá, the capital of Colombia. This tradition has been main-tained in a number of cities of Africa and the Middle East: Kano in Nigeria, Agadez in Niger, Tombouctou in Mali, Oualata in Mauritania, Marrakesh in Morocco, Adrar in Algeria, Ghadames in Libya, Sa'dah in North Yemen, Shibam in South Yemen and Yazd in Iran.

Earth architecture in rural communities has been still more widespread and varied, so that to list it would be tedious. Many familiar examples are to be found in Asia, Africa, the Middle East and Latin America, while those in Europe and the USA are less well known: there are thousands of earth buildings both in dry regions such as Spain and Italy and in rainy countries like England, Germany, Denmark and Sweden. In France, at least 15 per cent of rural buildings are still made of raw earth, and numerous examples survive near Lyons, Reims, Grenoble, Toulouse, Rennes, Avignon and even Chartres, close to Paris.

## The Tower of Babel

Unbaked earth has been used for thousands of years not only in rural housing, but also for the vast, prestigious monuments that reflect the material and spiritual development of communities – warehouses and aqueducts, ziggurats and pyramids, monasteries, churches and mosques. In these, mankind's creative drive seemed to reach its full expression. In the 7th century BC even the famous Tower of Babel was built of earth, its seventh level teetering at 90 m – mankind's first skyscraper. That record-breaking creation succumbed to the social chaos for which it has become the symbol, but the Great Wall of China, of which large parts are of unbaked earth, has managed to survive since the 3rd century BC, and testifies – as do many other monuments – to the enduring strength of this material. It is on account of these qualities that cities throughout the world have been protected by unbaked earth defences – from as early as the walls of Jericho, until 1882, when Tiznit, in Morocco, became perhaps the last city to be provided with earth ramparts.

Military strategists, too, have from ancient times recognized the virtues of earth as a strong and resistant building material. The Roman historian Pliny the Elder relates how in Spain, in about 219 BC, Hannibal constructed buildings out of unbaked earth; just as the American Army used it during the Second World War for the erection of dams, military camps and airstrips.

It is not only the world's decision-makers who appreciate the architectural qualities of unbaked earth, for the great majority of earth buildings have been, and still are, residential houses. These buildings come in a surprising variety of forms, each indicative of the cultural characteristics of their builders. All over the world, from Scandinavia to South Africa, earth constructions have been adapted to suit the most diverse types of climate. Wisely used, unbaked earth ensures optimal 'thermal comfort', providing natural regulation between indoor and outdoor temperatures, in sharp contrast to the heat-loss and overheating characteristics of other materials, and particularly concrete.

## Construction Methods

At least 20 different traditions of earth construction are known, but among these, two major processes predominate. The first is *pisé de terre* – a name of Latin origin first used in Lyons in 1562 – applied to the principle of constructing walls at least 50 cm thick by ramming earth between parallel frames that are then removed, revealing a completed section of hard earth wall. The second is *adobe* – an Arabic and Berber word brought by Spaniards to the Americas where it was adopted into English – applied to earth bricks shaped in moulds, dried in the sun and then used to build walls, vaults and domes. In both cases the earth is carefully selected; for adobe bricks, for instance, it is mixed with water and vegetable fibres (usually chopped straw) to form a cohesive mixture.

Ways have also been evolved over the centuries for counteracting erosion by water. The English have a concise expression for this empirical common sense: 'Give 'un a gude hat an' a gude pair o' butes an' er'll 'ast forever', which means simply that an earth house needs an overhanging roof to protect the walls from rain and stone foundations to protect the foot of the walls from running water and humidity. In addition, even 6000 years ago bitumen-based renderings were used to protect earth constructions. Like the Aztecs later, the Mesopotamians covered the external walls of large public buildings, temples and palaces with a facing which not only protected the raw earth from rain, but allowed geometrical and figurative motifs to be made of stones, baked bricks or polished ceramic cones, embedded in the walls during their construction.

## Spirituality and Sensuality

More modest dwellings are frequently protected by coatings which are themselves earth-based and which are renewed in an annual ritual after the rainy season. At such times, both the material and the spiritual aspects of the act of building become indissolubly linked, as each individual projects his personality into a rich variety of visual and tactile forms. The intense pleasure which traditional civilizations derive from manipulating the ornamentation and conveying their vital forces into plastic signs, is expressed in the artistic and decorative appearance of earth architecture. Engraved on the walls or applied in relief, it is in turn abstract, gestural, geometric, symbolic and figurative.

The modelling and sculpting of earth involves an entire spectrum of plastic languages, expressing man's most profound creative impulses. The erotic curves and sensuous forms reach their zenith in the sculptural earth architecture of certain cultures in Africa and the Middle East. For there, earth – the most fertile element of our planet – becomes a symbol of sexuality. Elsewhere architecture is more austere and virile, and the earth may acquire different values. In the case of multi-storeyed houses and minarets, heights of 30 m may be reached, in spectacular shows of primal force.

## Industrialization

But in our times the fate of earth architecture is being determined by unprecedented economic and demographic developments. Third World countries where earth is traditionally used continue to employ it. The predominantly poor, rural and isolated populations are rapidly expanding, and these inhabitants, robbed by dire poverty of their freedom of choice, are compelled to build in readily available local materials. Although in some regions the practice of earth construction is perceptibly on the decline, the overall picture remains stationary, if not perhaps even on the ascendant.

This is not the case in those countries recently enriched by the oil boom: there, earth construction has tended to disappear in the face of frenetic imitation of architectural stereotypes and technologies from the West. In New Mexico, California and other southern states, where the Indian and Spanish adobe native to the Southwest remained alive until the 19th century, the traditions have managed to survive the process of industrialization. On several occasions between 1890 and 1940, stylistic revivals either of the authentic material or of parodies of it guaranteed its perpetuation, until the energy crisis of 1973 stimulated a veritable renaissance of earth architecture especially in New Mexico.

Earth construction in European towns and cities – for example, at Lyons, France – was maintained until the end of the 19th century both by the working and the middle classes, while in the countryside it remained widespread until the Second World War. This same tradition was brought to Australia, where *pisé* and adobe appeared at the beginning of the 19th century and were widely applied and developed for a hundred years, benefitting from considerable research and technical improvements.

## Advocates and Improvements

The very first interest in earth architecture was aroused in Australia in 1823, in the USA in 1806 and in Denmark, Germany and Italy from 1790 onwards, in each case by the works of the French architect François Cointeraux, born in Lyons in 1740. He had invented, during the French Revolution of 1789, what he called the 'New *Pisé*',[1] aiming to have this analysis of the traditions of his own region accepted by the New France which was developing around him. He designed urban and rural houses adapted to different social classes, as well as structures intended to further the economic development of the country: from agricultural concerns to factories. For Cointeraux, 'the precious art of *pisé*' was 'for an enlightened nation, a sure way of making its countryside, its commerce and its industry prosperous.' Cointeraux went to extreme lengths to publicize his ideas and persuade people to adopt them, publishing over 50 works in the course of 22 years, in which he explained and justified his technological proposals.

## Cointeraux and Fathy: Waging the Same War

Cointeraux used every possible means to combat prejudices against earth architecture; and 116 years after his death the Egyptian architect Hassan Fathy launched a similar campaign in 1946. The lives and vocations of these two men are remarkably similar, for each observed the beginnings of the industrial era in his own country. Both tirelessly devoted a long life to the defence and revival of architectural forms rooted in the popular traditions of each country. Both became writers, both employing the theatre for polemical ends. One founded architectural schools in Grenoble and then in Paris, the other founded an International Institute for Research into Appropriate Technology. Both received patronage for a time from enlightened aristocrats: one from the Duke of Charost and the other from the Aga Khan.

Although neither had the opportunity to build much – by 1981 there remained only symbolic traces of the work of either – they were both invited abroad to demonstrate the qualities of the architecture they were promoting: in the early 19th century François Cointeraux went to England, and in 1981 Hassan Fathy visited the USA. And it was abroad that they gained their following and that their ideas had most impact. The common denominator of these pioneers from the West and the Third World is the incessant battle they waged against the prejudices of their contemporaries, and particularly those of politicians.

## Prejudices

An ancient pyramid seen by Rondelet near Cairo in the 19th century and said to have been built of raw earth by King Asychis, bore the following inscription at its base:

Despise me not in comparing me to pyramids of stone; I am as superior to them as Jupiter is to other gods; for I am of bricks made with mud from the bottom of the lake.

Since that time, prejudices have continued to flourish under many guises, condemning earth as poor, fragile, archaic and primitive. Yet evidence from all over the world points in precisely the opposite direction: that earth is a versatile building material with many qualities to commend its use today. Earth buildings are indeed highly susceptible to damage by water, but various remedies for this danger have been developed over the centuries, and many other modern processes have recently been perfected. These include, for example, the use of 'stabilized earth', whereby the earth is mixed with small quantities of other products such as bituminous residues or cement, thus considerably improving its resistance and impermeability. Simple manual and hydraulic machines now enable large numbers of bricks to be mass produced, and the products of such presses are also far more solid than those pressed by hand. Straw was often used as a binding material, but tests have shown that this could harbour insects and microbes. Modern bricks are therefore prepared by a process which eliminates the need for this.

Modern researchers have analysed scientifically those methods formerly employed intuitively, but they have also determined how to improve both the selection of components and the quantities used. The techniques of *pisé* construction have also been refined by the introduction of machines which compress the earth pneumatically and are far faster and more powerful than manual methods ever were. The current tendency, therefore, is to combine the merits of traditional principles and modern expertise, and thereby to achieve the best possible results. Work is also under way in Peru and the USA on systems of building in earth which minimize the effects of earthquakes.

## The Opposition

Although unbaked earth no longer needs any real justification on technical or material grounds, resistance to it persists from quarters whose economic, psychological, cultural, institutional and political well-being is threatened by it. Such opposition is sometimes calculatingly self-interested, for the economic systems characteristic of earth construction might injure influential interest-groups. Industrial corporations and multi-nationals which produce building materials, as well as the technical consultants responsible for employing them, occasionally seek to discredit unbaked earth in order to protect their own markets. By making predominant use of cement, steel, aluminium and oil-derivatives for over half a century, conventional architecture has encouraged the growth of industrial monopolies. Their dependence leads them to favour these markets, even though the plants that produce the materials have a renowned capacity for devouring energy and causing pollution.

When the Chinese set up a network of 3000 small cement-factories, with one in almost every commune which between them accounted for two-thirds of the national production, India recently hoped to decentralize in a similar way. Georges Fernandes, the Minister of Industry, however, says that this 'was sabotaged by the interests of big capital'.[2] It is unfortunately characteristic that attempts to exploit materials democratically by producing them regionally are blocked because of the primacy of the economic domain over the political one. In Tanzania and several other Third World countries, cement is two or three times more expensive in the countryside than in the city where it is produced. In Jamaica the energy used in the 'local' production of cement accounts for 60 per cent of the material's value. These constraints, created by modern technology, inhibit Third

World countries from finding even the beginnings of a realistic solution to the rapidly growing problem of basic housing. Yet the number of houses needed there in the next 20 years approaches the astounding figure of 500 million.

## Financial Considerations

Various 'development banks' set up to help poorer countries overcome their economic difficulties might, one would have hoped, have taken a realistic approach to the challenges facing the world today. But it was revealed in a recent enquiry[3] that in the key area of producing building materials 'practically all the financial negotiations and loans concern heavy cement-works only'. Some aid-organizations recognize their own shortcomings in this respect: the European Development Fund, for example, admits that it has made excessive use of expensive high technology materials such as steel and cement in Africa. Since then it has successfully experimented with modes of construction involving, in particular, unbaked earth. An example of this is the health centre at Mopti in Mali, designed by the French architect André Ravereau and the Belgian architect Philippe Lauwers (see pp. 158–9). Other institutions such as the World Bank seem to contradict their own aims, however, for although that organization theoretically encourages self-help housing and gives priority to the need to satisfy requirements in the Third World, observers 'sought in vain to find the slightest evidence of loans destined for research into production methods based on alternative technologies related to construction materials'.[4]

These trends only serve to foster one of the major dilemmas of our time: the deepening poverty of the poor and increasing prosperity of the rich. These effects often result from excessive optimism about the resources of Western technologies, yet they also arise from a failure to take account of an unquantifiable but powerful cultural dimension. The violence of the cultural revolution in Iran since 1980 and its international repercussions have led powers such as the World Bank and Saudi Arabia to include this factor in their calculations. Is it by chance that these giants have recently commissioned research into earth-architecture, an area which seemed of no interest to them a short while ago?

## The Washing-Line Paradox

These mental blocks also exist among groups of people who ought to know better. A few architects and even more engineers respond with contempt to suggestions of building in unbaked earth. Although this was never discussed with them during their formative years and is therefore unfamiliar, a more powerful disincentive is the convention of calculating their fees according to the overall cost of the work: a strong argument against researching into economical alternatives. For similar reasons, the major professional institutions, insurance companies and public authorities – who establish the norms – are often so blind to the realities of contemporary society that adobe or pisé do not so much as figure on their lists of approved (or even existing) building materials. This is despite the fact that more than one-third of the world's population uses this material for shelter.

Yet there too, one detects signs of change as the technocratic grip gradually loosens. The frequent failure of 'development' programmes has prompted a more modest and realistic approach. For only recently, rapid and full-scale mechanization was still considered the key to the agricultural development of the Third World, and essential for the survival of the human race. Nevertheless, a United Nations conference at Nairobi in 1981, on renewable forms of energy, was told that 92 per cent of agricultural traction is still provided by animals, and that only optimists see this dropping to 80 per cent by the year 2000. Indeed, the role of tractors seems derisory in comparison with that of 400 million animals. The same goes for construction in unbaked earth. It is either illusory or dishonest to pretend that one can do without basic, traditional materials, so often overlooked in economic accounts and planning.

Paradoxically, it is precisely those most economical and efficient aspects of society that usually escape the calculators of Gross National Product. The American architect Steve Baer has formulated the 'washing-line paradox' – the energy-saving made by drying washing in the sun is ignored, while people using electric driers are considered to be constributing to the 'material wellbeing' of the country! The millions of families who build their own homes in earth each year are similarly ignored because they do not consume according to the norms of industrial production.

## Political Decisions

Political decisions are essential if these views are to be effectively countered, as has been clearly demonstrated in the case of solar energy. Politicians vacillated at first between timorous gestures and ambitious programmes, but encouragement from the government rapidly changed the situation in England, where in 1970 there were no solar-heating firms, while 8 years later there were 70. France could claim only one small company attempting to promote unbaked earth housing in 1981,[5] one architectural school which since 1979 had been carrying out full-time research into this material[6] and one firm which began to manufacture unbaked earth bricks.[7] In France, there were thousands of workers 40 years ago who could build in *pisé*, but with them this knowledge has died, as it has in other countries.

In the Third World a political awareness of the potential of architecture in unbaked earth is beginning to crystallize. This is due, firstly, to growing doubts about the economic implications of the excessive importation of construction materials, which represented 2.6% of the total Gross National Product of African countries in 1965, and 3.6% in 1972 (5% and 8% of the total value of goods imported into Africa).[8] Secondly, it results from a realization of the enormous cost in terms of energy consumption both during and after construction, and of the political implications of the financial dependence which this reinforces. A third factor is primarily social: Western forms of technology are not only expensive to buy and to use, but are also designed to reduce manual labour to a minimum, emphasizing the role of capital. In poorer countries, however, it is labour that is increasingly underemployed, while local capital remains weak.

The solution, then, is the establishment of many inexpensive construction sites which also create jobs. This has been done in China with the construction of earth dams (on the same lines as that at Serre-Ponçon in the Alps), or in Morocco between 1963 and 1966 with the construction of a complex of 3200 very economical earth houses in Marrakesh, by a workforce consisting of 90 per cent unemployed and unskilled, and 10 per cent skilled workers. In China, construction sites have been given clearly defined political themes, such as 'We must rely on our own resources'; and similar points were made in East Germany from 1946 to 1958 during the construction of thousands of villages and towns in unbaked earth, as well as in Peru since the 1960s.

In many other countries, however, we find evidence only of short-lived programmes initiated by a few experts, or mounted in order to attract financial aid which is often then channelled away from its original destination. But on the other hand, declarations have recently been made by certain heads of state which confirm the cultural significance of basic political and economic choices concerning architectural production.

Anicet Kashamura, the Minister of Information in Zaire in 1971, declared:

For us Africans, certain cultural principles must change. We must choose what has to be conserved, adapted and handed on. We must choose between utopia and realism. We must escape the misfortunes which menace the so-called civilized societies. We must dispense with the principles of imperialism and colonialism in the name of alleged 'humanism' and 'progress'. I recognize, with René Dumont, that *Africa has got off to a bad start*,[9] but I do not think that her future has already been lost.[10]

Mrs Indira Gandhi, Prime Minister of India, stated in 1980:

All the new houses are built for energy consumption. They are hot in summer and cold in winter, whereas our old houses are not. So we have not only to have new technology, but look a bit to the old technology. There is much sense in what people have evolved over the years to suit their climate, their environment, their way of living. You can't keep all of it, because our way of life has changed, but I think a lot of it can be adapted and made more efficient.[11]

Finally, Julius Nyerere, President of the Republic of Tanzania, declared in 1977:

People refuse to build a house of burned bricks and tiles; they insist on waiting for a tin roof and 'European soil' – cement. If we want to progress more rapidly in the future we must overcome at least some of these mental blocks.[12]

## Doubts

In the West, this new awareness is more scattered and the problems partly different. A number of intellectuals have been advancing new points of view, some of which are gradually being assimilated into institutional organizations. These include the theories expressed by Dr E. F. Schumacher, whose concept of 'appropriate technology', originally expressed in 1963 and published in *Small is Beautiful* in 1973, has been digested and partly applied by the World Bank. Even Prince Charles in 1981 referred to Dr E. F. Schumacher's slogan in an interview about the future of British industry.[13] Few and far between are those men who, like John Turner working in Peru, the USA and England, and Hassan Fathy in Egypt, have linked a strategy for development with the modernization of earth architecture. Intellectual pioneers such as Ivan Illich and Dr Schumacher blaze new trails, but it takes time for their thinking to filter down to the institutions responsible for development. None other than Nicolas Jéquier, principal administrator of the Development Center at the OECD, testifies:

Appropriate technology can be considered to be one of the expressions of a cultural revolution. Our societies, be they industrialized or in the process of developing, require new types of technology and this change has been quite brutal since it has occurred over the space of half a decade, that is, symbolically, between the riots of May 1968 and the oil-crisis of October 1973. The technological system has not yet managed to keep pace with this change of attitudes and today one is confronted with an enormous potential demand and a dramatically insufficient supply.

## Technological Optimism and Disillusion

On the other hand, it has been known for people to perform a complete volte-face, as in the case of Owings, the American architect who as co-founder of one of the world's largest multinational architectural agencies – Skidmore, Owings and Merrill – is often considered a symbol of the 'International Style'. When he built his *own* house, however, he adopted an opposite approach and chose to make it of unbaked earth, declaring: 'This house is built in natural materials rather than processed materials. You can build a perfectly good adobe house without using any metals. My reaction is to go violently far from the mechanical aspects of the modern scene.'[14]

Such disillusionment with heavy technology became common in the West during the 1970s, for technological optimism looks harder to justify after a perusal of the balance-sheet; and this enlightenment has provoked a gradual abandonment of megalomaniac projects such as giant dams and oil-tankers. 'Modernity at any price' can entail an incalculable cost in social terms, and the 'functionalism' which we praised so highly and for which we paid so dearly often turned out to be highly inefficient in certain contexts. Since then, we have learned to see the frantic race for 'progress' as irresponsible, and all the more so since it may lead to the destruction of traditions: a cultural 'scorched earth' strategy. In their euphoria, many decision-makers believed they could dispense with tradition, and drive us into a state of amnesia. But the consequences of these errors have been heavy, and certain leaders are now preparing to take action.

Half a century after the use of sails had been abandoned for commercial shipping in the West, three great industrial powers – the USA, Japan and France – started reviving this ancient tradition and exploiting it commercially; and not out of nostalgia, but for reasons of efficiency, economy, technological realism and political responsibility. The fishing-boat *Eole* was launched in France in 1981, and the small oil-carrier *Shin Aitoku Maru* in Japan in 1980, both of them examples of the same approach: the revival of the ancient principles of harnessing wind-power combined with the latest technical knowledge. Sails of metal or textile are adjusted by computers to ensure that the wind and a complementary motor are used to the best effect. So far, energy savings of 50 per cent have been achieved, opening the way to still more effective projects.

## Autonomy

This synthesis between 'traditional' and 'modern' techniques amounts to a completely new approach, in which methods are both more appropriate to our own needs, and place us in a position to master the tool rather than to be mastered by it. In the field of housing in the West, we are seeking to debureaucratize and democratize what should be a shared cultural initiative. Therefore, in the USA, 160,000 houses were built annually by the occupants themselves in the years around 1970,[15] and in 1980 in New Mexico half the adobe bricks produced were made by the users, who built their own homes without any outside help. Such forms of social organization have often been neglected in the course of Western-style industrialization.

The autonomy of the user, who may be a local collective or a whole society, is more than a means to an end. For by being able to determine his own relationship to local resources and requirements, the human being recovers his 'conviviality', in the meaning coined by Ivan Illich when he says: 'The tool is convivial in that everyone can use it without difficulty, as often or as rarely as he wishes, to ends which he defines himself. . . . It does not encroach upon the liberty of the other to do the same. It acts as a conductor of mutual understanding and an interpretor of intentions between man and the world.' Viewed in this way, earth architecture is not merely an economic expediency, but a social force with incalculably beneficial effects.

## Neither Dominated nor Dominating

The clays and lateritic soils suitable for use in buildings constitute 74 per cent of the earth's crust,[16] and therefore rarely need to be purchased or transported to where they are needed. This frequently releases the user from the constraints of commercial monopoly, and permits production to take place in decentralized enterprises which do not cause pollution. To this extent, the use of earth requires neither an economy which dominates nor one which is dominated, and this guarantees the maintenance of ecological equilibria; while in the social sphere, the variety of ways this material can be used enables one to choose between large but not very specialized workforces such as the family unit, and far more complex procedures. Owner-builder construction helps to relieve unemployment, restores the democratic dimension to planning and helps reduce social inequalities by eliminating the need for economic intermediaries. It is a powerful reinforcer of the autonomy of the individual, of the group or of the nation.

## The Spirit of Place

In addition to its political, economic, social and ecological advantages, earth has great cultural and architectural importance. The wide variety of ways of building in earth represents a guarantee against cultural imperialism, such as the imposition of a uniform idea like the 'International Style' – once lauded as being suitable for anywhere and everywhere – from which we have now begun to escape over the last few years. Earth could also promote the reintegration of architecture into cultural and popular traditions from which it has been excluded, reconciling us with the nature of each region and recreating a comprehensible link between the past and the future. We can now see hospitals and schools, dams and factories, hotels and museums, apartment blocks and villas, housing projects and villages, all constructed in raw earth. These provide living evidence of a renaissance in earth architecture both in the public and the private domains, and in Europe and the USA as well as the Third World. In America, indeed, where this phenomenon has intensified since the energy crisis, half the total output of adobe bricks in New Mexico in 1980 was assured by some 50 light-industrial production units, and the other half by the users themselves.

## Energy Saving

The savings in energy to be made both during and after construction in unbaked earth can be calculated when we consider that in the West, the energy used in industrial and domestic construction can represent from 20 to 25 per cent of a nation's total energy consumption. Earth bricks are not baked – a process entailing ovens heated to between $900^\circ$ and $1100^\circ$ C – and they need little if any transportation, since they are produced on site or locally.

In addition to energy savings at the production stage, unbaked-earth buildings also require less heating and cooling, for the earth walls ensure a substantial reduction in heat-loss and a general feeling of what is called 'thermal comfort'. This factor cannot be quantified, but it helps to explain the cultural nature of the process by which some members of society – often the more privileged – appreciate the comfortable, secure and ecological aspects of unbaked earth, while others – often the poorer – frequently feel that earth entraps them within an archaism which they perceive as an obstacle to attaining their social aspirations: to become ostentatious consumers in the true style of modern 'progress'.

## North-South Dialogues and 'Eco-Developments'

Research on earth building is currently being carried out by small decentralized teams in a number of places. Far from being isolationist, with several groups reinventing everything alone, each autonomous study is complemented and enriched by copious but selective exchange with the outside world. The issue of earth architecture is vital and decisive: it provides the key to progress from 'bad development' to 'eco-development'. Yet in this atmosphere of open communication between different areas of the world, scepticism remains as to what the West could gain from technological experiments undertaken in the Third World. Let us consider just two examples. The first is a simple machine for making bricks in stabilized earth – the 'Cinva-Ram' press – invented and patented in Colombia in 1957, and commercialized throughout the world mainly by a French firm who acquired the partial licence for manufacturing it. The second example is a Danish programme for exploiting the energy resources of 'bio-gas' released in the treatment of organic waste. This form of 'appropriate technology' was introduced into Denmark by engineers from India who had been conducting similar experiments there, originally inspired by work carried out in China in about 1958. Denmark perhaps leads the West in the practice of 'intermediate' and 'soft' technology, for there it forms part of a well-established political and cultural

tradition: it was in that country that François Cointeraux most quickly established a following, and one still finds tens of thousands of houses built in raw earth during the 19th century.

A North–South dialogue, between countries on the road to industrialization and those moving away from it, does not imply a unilateral flow of ideas, however. It is in the Third World that the spiritual, cultural and artistic traditions of earth architecture are threatened with disappearance while still surviving, whereas the West is perfecting ways of modernizing this material technologically and combining its use with that of solar energy and other bio-climatic principles, themselves frequently based on traditional common sense. Since the petrol crisis of 1973, houses have been built which demonstrate an extraordinary level of energy self-sufficiency, some providing up to 95 per cent of domestic needs. These 'solaradobe' constructions are one of the major areas of experimentation in the architecture of the future.

## A New Future?

Earth architecture should not, of course, be considered a miraculous solution to all our housing problems, nor one which can be applied successfully anywhere and everywhere. We have suffered sufficiently from a succession of messianic calls – 'all coal', 'all oil', 'all electric' and 'all nuclear' – to have learnt to avoid the temptation of these awesome, all-encompassing and unrealistic schemes. The idea of 'all earth' would be equally erroneous, and, indeed, no more need be said than that earth architecture is ready for a new lease of life and a new future.

Forthcoming developments will be especially exciting to watch, since they will be directly linked to interactions between highly unpredictable factors – economic, industrial, political, cultural, social and psychological. The unbaked-earth phenomenon represents one of those paradoxical twists of history: we are witnessing the potential enrichment of our future thanks to skills invented almost 10,000 years ago, handed down to us across the centuries enshrined in the popular traditions of pre-industrial societies.

JEAN DETHIER

## NOTES

1 The *Nouveau Pisé* ('New *Pisé*') invented by Cointeraux consisted of unbaked earth bricks compressed by means of a mechanical press which he patented under the name of 'la Crécise'. As these bricks were meticulously finished and quite large he called them 'artificial bricks'.

2 Cited by Anil Agarwal in *Mud, Mud: The potential of earth-based materials for Third World housing* (London, International Institute for Environment and Development, (Earthscan) 1981).

3 Stuart Donelson, Jorge E. Hardoy and Susana Schkolnick, *Aid for Human Settlements* (London, International Institute for Environment and Development, 1978).

4 *Ibid.*

5 The company 'Terre et Soleil' ('Earth and Sun') run by Mr Pedrotti in Lyons.

6 The architectural school at Grenoble where the CRATerre group conducts a regular course and research work into unbaked earth.

7 The company of Chaffoteaux and Maury commercializes bricks and tiles in stabilized earth under the name of 'Stargil', made according to the patented research of the *Institut National des Sciences Appliquées* ('National Institute for Applied Sciences') at Rennes. The *Centre Technique des Tuiles et Briques* ('Technical Center for Tiles and Bricks') in Paris have also been attempting since 1979 to achieve energy savings of 50 per cent by manufacturing these products in raw earth.

8 *Human Settlements in Africa* (United Nations, Economic Commission for Africa, Addis-Ababa, 1976).

9 René Dumont, the ecologist and former candidate for the French presidency, published a highly polemical book in 1962 entitled *L'Afrique noire est mal partie*.

10 Anicet Kashamura, *Culture et aliénation en Afrique* (Editions du Cercle, Paris, 1971).

11 'Taking an all-round Attitude to Science', interview with Indira Gandhi (*Nature*, Vol. 285, no. 5761, London, 1980).

12 Julius Nyerere, *The Arusha Declaration: Ten Years After* (Tanzania Publishing House, Dar es Salaam, 1977).

13 Interview with Prince Charles by Rosemary Bailey, printed in *Engineering Today* (London, November 1981) and *The Sunday Times* (London, 22 November 1981).

14 *Architectural Forum* (New York, September 1972, pp. 42–5).

15 William C. Grindley, 'Owners-Builders: Survivors with a future', in *Freedom to Build*, ed. John Turner and Robert Fichter (New York, Macmillan, 1972).

16 According to Hugo Houben and Patrice Doat of the CRATerre group.

# Architecture in Earth: Historical and Popular Traditions

Our purpose in this book is not to present a nostalgic roll-call of architectural forms from the past for complacent and passive contemplation. On the contrary, our aim is to argue realistically in favour of unbaked earth for construction purposes in both industrialized countries and in the so-called Third World.

This approach forms part of a new current of opinion in architectural practice. For the discipline has undergone a major change since the 1970s: at last we have recognized a fundamental historical error on which the dogma of orthodox contemporary architecture was based for half a century. From the 1920s onwards it came to be believed that if we were to achieve 'modernity', all reference to history and tradition must be totally obliterated. This arrogant principle was put into effect on a scale for which we find no precedent in history. It has led to the creation of a physical and cultural environment profoundly unsuited to both the material and emotional needs of many of the societies involved. This violation of the collective memory acquired over centuries has established an abyss of incomprehension mixed with conflict, between the decision-makers on the one hand and the users of architecture on the other, between technology and society.

More recently, however, young architects have begun to find ways of overcoming this deep-seated state of cultural amnesia; they are attempting to rediscover and reinterpret some of the lessons of historical and popular traditions, swept aside to make way for the 'International Style' imposed upon us by purveyors of cultural totalitarianism. We now see that if we wish the planning of our environment to be as democratic as our governments it is vital that we once more grant the inhabitants of any locale their right to have a memory.

It is in keeping with this spirit that we have chosen to devote a large part of this book to illustrations of traditional architecture, drawn from about 40 countries in 5 continents. The best way of forming an idea of what *can* be constructed in unbaked earth seemed to be to examine what people actually *had* built with it in the past, and what many continue to create every day. To fulfil this two-fold requirement, the first section of this book portrays the architectural products of ancient civilizations – these are by way of historical references – and the second records popular traditions still practised by urban and rural groups in the 20th century, indicating that this heritage is both thriving and evolving.

Most traditional housing in the Third World presented here was built only a few years ago. In southern Morocco, for example, the custom of building in earth still abounds, although this has sometimes been modified to suit a Western model. In their own way, therefore, these traditional constructions are completely contemporary.

# 1 Man's Oldest Building Material

In order to discover the origins of building in unbaked earth, we must look back some 10,000 years to the Near East, where men first assembled in villages. The earliest of these appears to have been Jericho. Like Jericho, the famous city of Babylon was built in raw earth, as was the monument which dominated its heart some 27 centuries ago: the Tower of Babel. Since that time the practice of building in unbaked earth has remained widespread in most countries of the world. Nowadays, at least a third of the world's population still lives in houses of earth, benefitting from the efforts of countless generations of urban or rural peoples who, constantly assimilating, reinventing, and improving these building techniques, handed their knowledge on to their successors. Earth construction has passed the test of time, proving its merits and adaptability to the most diverse cultures, geographical conditions and climates.

Examples of earth architecture are to be found in every continent: not only in the form of historical and archaeological remains but also, and above all, in the innumerable towns and villages where the secular heritage, enriched by exchanges between the most varied civilizations, is perpetuated daily. Recent developments such as the energy crisis seem to invite us to continue this vital cycle of renewal of earth architecture.

24

**Double page** Air-view of the center of a village in the Dra valley, Morocco. (Photo by Pierre Moreau, 1970)

**1** The rite of making the first brick in unbaked earth, from a Pharaonic frieze in the Temple of Montu, at Tod, Egypt. (Photo by Christine Bastin, 1980)

**2** Reconstruction of an Inca villa in the Rimac valley near Lima, Peru. (Photo by Richard List, 1978)

**3** Reconstruction of the temple of Emach, built in about 1968 in Iraq. (Photo by André Stevens, 1979; *see* p. 136, ill. 8)

**4** Part of the necropolis of Bagawat, built some 1500 years ago at the el-Kharga oasis in Egypt. (Photo by Jacques Evrard, 1980)

**5** Towns in the ancient Middle East were probably similar to the fortified settlement of Tissergate in the Dra valley, Morocco. (Photo by Christian Lignon, 1981)

**6** Bas-relief of an ancient town in Mesopotamia. (Photo by Anne Moreau)

**7** Part of a strip cartoon by Jacques Martin, entitled 'The Prince of the Nile', showing an Egyptian town with houses of unbaked earth built around a palace. (Photo courtesy of Casterman Editions, Paris/Tournai)

**8** Remains of a *stupa* (a funerary monument) built in the 6th or 7th century in the Turfan region of China. (Photo by André Stevens, 1981)

**9** Many civilizations have constructed pyramids with bricks of unbaked earth, often coating the structure with a weatherproof skin. This method was employed by the Pharaohs in Egypt, the Aztecs and the Toltecs in Mexico, and the Mochica civilization in Peru. (Photo by Christine Bastin, 1980)

**10** This structure of unbaked earth, built by Indians in about 1350, is one of the oldest architectural monuments in North America. The ruins of the 'Casa Grande' (Arizona), an important part of the American historical and cultural heritage, are now protected by a metallic canopy. (Photo by Christine Bastin, 1981)

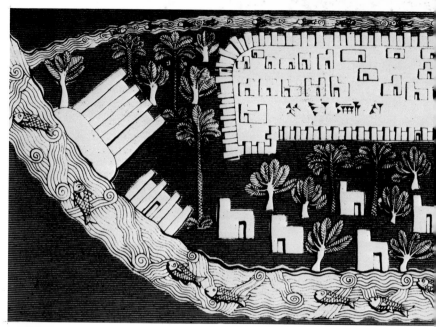

I

# 2  Strength and Durability

Although popular traditions of building in unbaked earth are known to have an ancient heritage, prejudices persist against earth constructions, based on the claim that they are fragile and unable to withstand the tests of time. To prove how strong and resistant they are if well designed, one need only point to ancient buildings still standing all over the world. The facts are more eloquent than words.

In Asia, long stretches of the Great Wall of China begun in the 3rd century BC are composed principally of earth. In North Africa, similarly, the fortified walls of the largest and most beautiful imperial cities in Morocco – Rabat, Marrakesh, Fes and Meknes – were created in raw earth beginning in the 12th century. Various examples are to be found in Europe, including the famous Alhambra begun in the 13th century in Granada in Spain, the center of Milton Abbas built in 1773 in Dorset, England, numerous castles and churches of the 13th century built in the Dauphiné and Burgundy regions of France, and the center of the town of Weilburg, built in the 19th century near Frankfurt in Germany. In America, the centers of cities founded during the period of Spanish domination beginning in the 16th century often contain buildings of raw earth. This is true of Bogotá, the capital of Colombia, and Santa Fe, the capital of New Mexico. Outside the urban centers of the American Southwest, there are many examples of churches and monasteries constructed in adobe in the 17th and 18th centuries. These buildings all testify, each in its own way, to the durability of the material of which they are built: unbaked earth.

28

**1** Mosque of Djenne, in Mali, rebuilt in 1905. (Photo by Yvette Vincent-Alleaume, 1974)

**2** Defensive entrance of Bab-al-Idriss at Al-Shihr, South Yemen. (Photo by Jean Gire)

**3** Fortified church of the Isleta Pueblo, built around 1680 by the Spanish in New Mexico. (Photo by Christine Bastin, 1981)

**4** Main entrance of the great Friday Mosque, at Mopti in Mali, rebuilt in 1935. (Photo by Sergio Domian, 1981)

**5** Ramparts of Tashkurgam in Afghanistan. (Photo by Roland Michaud/Rapho)

**6** Fortified village of Bololag in Afghanistan. (Photo by Paolo Koch/Rapho)

**7** Ramparts of Marrakesh in Morocco, built in the 13th century and classed as a historic monument in 1922. (Photo by Christian Lignon, 1981)

**8** Air-view of Tiznit in Morocco, first built in 1882 and surrounded by 5 km of defensive walls in *pisé*. (Photo by Pierre Moreau, 1970)

I

2

# 3 Variety of Forms

Unbaked earth is a simple and obvious building material, not least since it constitutes 74 per cent of the world's crust. With it, societies throughout the world have produced an extraordinary range of architectural languages, each eloquently proclaiming the cultural characteristics of its users. The spirit of place and community is fully expressed in these buildings, whose subtle variations are adapted to specific social and economic, geographical and climatic environments.

The intelligence and virtuosity of these traditions, however, have been brutally obscured and despised for over half a century. Influential voices called for 'progress at any price', which they claimed was embodied in the 'International Style' of architecture. By promoting this for all peoples in all climes, they ruthlessly ignored and erased regional traditions and ushered in an era of contempt for traditional expertise and of cultural amnesia. These traditions, however, constitute a heritage which we must now rediscover: not just out of nostalgia, but in order to recreate a living synthesis between the wisdom of the past and the knowledge of the future.

5

6

7

1 Communal dwelling-house for un-married men of the Bozo tribe, in a village near Mopti in Mali, built around 1850. (Photo by Sergio Domian, 1981)

2 Mausoleum of the prophet Hüd, at Qabr Hüd in South Yemen. (Photo by Christian Darles and Jean-François Breton)

3 Friday Mosque at San in Mali. Its three minarets date from about 1930. (Photo by Marli Shamir, 1970)

4 Courtyard of the mosque in the village of Igoulmine, near Goulmina in the Gheris valley, Morocco. (Photo by Christian Lignon, 1981)

5 Fortified farm – or 'tata' – of the Somba tribe, at Tapyeta in the region of Atakora, northwest Benin. (Photo by Bruno Français, 1981)

6 Town house at Segou in Mali. (Photo by Michel Renaudeau, 1981)

7 Town house at Mopti in Mali, built about 1960. (Photo by Sergio Domian, 1981)

8 Fortified farm – or 'kasbah' – in the Dades valley, Morocco. (Photo by Karl-Heinz Striedter)

12

13

14

**9** Traditional farm in the Dauphiné region of France. (Photo by Patrice Doat and Hugo Houben, 1978)

**10** House of a local notable in North Yemen. (Photo by Dominique Champault, Musée de l'Homme, Paris)

**11** Rural houses of the Aït Oudinar, built around 1960 in the Dades gorges in Morocco. (Photo by Christian Lignon, 1981)

**12** Rural dwelling – called *case-obus*, or 'shell-shaped hut', by the French – belonging to the Mousgoum tribe in the Cameroons. (Photo by Dominique Pidance and Alain Le Balh, 1979)

**13** Church of St Francis of Assisi, founded by Spanish missionaries in North America in 1782. It gave its name to the California city built around it – San Francisco. (Photo by Jacques Evrard, 1981)

**14** Pigeon-house in the Faiyum region of Egypt. (Photo by Jacques Evrard, 1981)

**15** Town house at Zinder in Niger. (Photo by René Gardi)

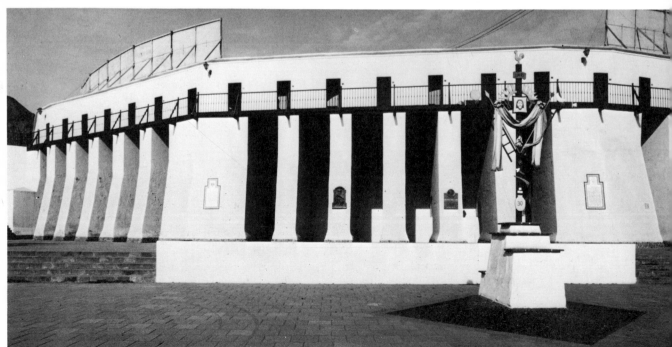

# 4  Its Many Uses

We are now so used to believing in the supremacy of modern orthodox architecture of the last 50 years that we overlook how traditional communities resolved, without any modern materials, all the architectural problems encountered previously. Earth architecture usually conjures up condescending images of 'primitive huts' and 'distant squalor', but if we look beyond such bigotry the reality looks very different. Firstly, dwellings built in earth throughout the world demonstrate a unique richness of design, technical ingenuity and subtle creativity. Secondly, this material has been used not only in houses, but in a great range of public and private buildings that reflect the grandeur and sophistication of urban and rural communities – mosques, churches, granaries, warehouses, ramparts, citadels, aqueducts, arenas, monumental gates, temples and palaces – all have been built in this most simple of materials.

3

**1** Ice-house in the Kermān region of Iran. (Photo by Bruno Barbey/Magnum)

**2** Bullfight arena built in the 18th century in Peru. (Photo by Ovidio Oré, 1981)

**3** The church of Bourdenous near Corbelin (in Ain), France. (Photo by Patrice Doat and Hugo Houben, 1976)

**4** Buildings for drying and storing grapes in the Turfan oasis, Sinkiang, China. (Photo by André Stevens, 1981)

**5** Grain silo in the Bandiagara region of Mali. (Photo by Yvette Vincent-Alleaume, 1974)

**6** The mosque of Kawara, north of Ferkessédougou, Ivory Coast. (Photo by René Gardi, 1975)

**7** Rural house at Djoub-es-Safa, 25 km east of Aleppo, Syria. (Photo by André Stevens, 1978)

**8** Boarding school, built in the 19th century in Lima, Peru. (Photo by Ovidio Oré, 1981)

**9** Water-tower and ducts at Ain Salah in the Algerian Sahara. (Photo by Anne Rochette, 1980)

**10** Monumental entrance to the town of Timimoun in the Algerian Sahara, dating from about 1930. (Photo by Bruno Français, 1981)

4

5

6

7

8

9

# 5 Earth Architecture the World Over

Traditional architecture in unbaked earth is found not only in the distant cultures of Africa. It is universal. Today we still find earth constructions in almost every country of the world: a kaleidoscopic variety of forms that has evolved over the centuries to suit innumerable cultures and climates from the arid semi-deserts of the South to the cold, rainy countries of the North. There is a continuous tradition of it from Scandinavia to South Africa, that passes through England, Germany, France, Spain and Italy, the Maghreb, the Sahara and west, east and central Africa. Similar forms of architecture thrive in North and Latin America, the Middle East, Asia and Australia. This simple material has proved astonishingly adaptable, and is still perfectly well suited to the technical and cultural needs of different urban and rural communities.

3

4

**1** Fortified rural dwelling – 'kasbah' – in the Imilchil region of the High Atlas mountains, Morocco. (Photo by David Hicks)

**2** Spanish village built of earth. (Photo by David Hicks)

**3** Rural houses at Gharb Aswan in Egypt. (Photo by Christine Bastin, 1980)

**4** Rural houses in India (Photo by Claude Sauvageot)

**5** Rural dwelling in Nepal. (Photo by Jean-Marc Charles/Rapho, 1976)

**6** Group of rural houses of the Aït Ibrirn, in the gorges of the Dades valley, Morocco. (Photo by Christian Lignon, 1981)

**7** Bank headquarters in the central square of Villa de Leyva, Colombia. (Photo by Ignacio Gomez-Pulido, 1977)

**8** Rural dwellings at K'un-ming, in the Yunnan province of China. (Photo courtesy of the Musée de l'Homme, Paris)

**9** Church of Santo Antonio, built around 1640 at São Roque in the state of São Paulo, Brazil. (Photo by Hélène Cassignol, 1981)

**10** Town houses at Djenne in Mali. (Photo by Marli Shamir, 1964)

**11** Town houses at Bukhara, in the Republic of Uzbekistan in the USSR. (Photo by Anne Salaun/Roger Viollet, 1969)

**12** Town houses at San'a in North Yemen. (Photo by Michel Andrault, 1975)

**13** Cottages of cob – earth on a rubble base – in Devon, southwest England. (Photo by David Hicks)

**14** The great mosque at Bobo Dioulasso, Upper Volta. (Photo by Don Foresta)

**15** Tiered houses of the Taos Pueblo, founded c. 1250 in New Mexico. (Photo by Jacques Evrard, 1981)

II

I

# 6  Construction Methods

Many ways of building in earth have been
evolved over the centuries, but two processes
have established themselves as the most
common and reliable: adobe and *pisé*.

Adobe – a word of Arab origin later adopted
in Spain and then in the Americas – is the name
of a technique in which earth mixed with water
and finely chopped straw is manually rammed
into wooden brick-moulds. These large bricks
are then left to dry in the sun for several days,
before being used to build walls, vaults and
domes. Ways have recently been devised of
accelerating and improving this production
method – including mechanic or hydraulic
manual presses (such as the 'Cinva-Ram' press
invented in Colombia in 1957 by Raoul Ramirez) and massive, semi-industrialized plants
such as the great mobile machines developed in
California by Hans Sumpf, each of which can
manufacture 15,000 adobes per day. These
adobes are nowadays often 'stabilized' by the
addition of a little cement (3–4%) which
greatly improves their resistance.

*Pisé*, or 'rammed earth', first appeared in
France in 1562 and consists of earth compressed between parallel wooden plates that
are removed to reveal a section of completed
wall, generally 50 cm thick. The wooden
boards are then set up further along so that
work can begin on another section of wall.
Traditionally the earth was compressed manually with heavy wooden hammers, but this can
now be accomplished more easily and rapidly
with pneumatic rammers. These improvements make it possible to use both adobe and
*pisé* on a large scale with the minimum of
mechanization.

2

3

6a

6b

6c

6d

7a

7b

7c

7d

8

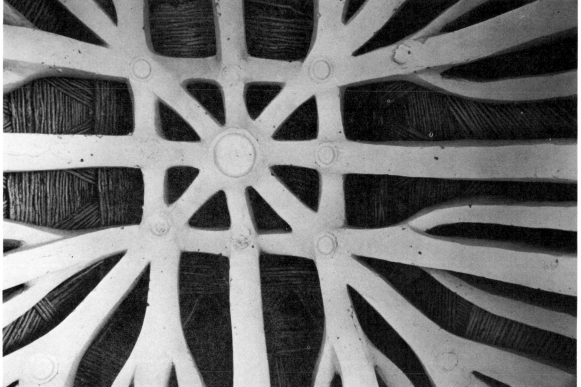

9

64

**1** Annual re-coating of the mosque of Koundouga, Upper Volta. (Photo by Jacques Evrard, 1978)

**2** Stele showing a Mesopotamian king participating symbolically in the first stages of the construction of a temple, by carrying a basketful of unbaked earth bricks on his head. (Photo courtesy of the Trustees of the British Museum, London)

**3** Statuette of a Mesopotamian worker carrying earth for brick-making. (Photo courtesy of the Trustees of the British Museum, London)

**4** How to make *pisé*: ramming the earth into lateral wooden frames, which are then removed to expose the hard wall. (Photo taken in Morocco by Dominique Pidance and Alain Le Bahl, 1980)

**5** Adobe: moulding unbaked earth bricks and drying them in the sun. (Photo taken in Algeria by Gérard Degeorges)

**6** Stages in constructing an oblique 'Nubian vault' out of unbaked earth bricks, without the use of centring:

  **a** The wall supporting the vault. (Photo taken in Iran by Bernard Gardi)

  **b** A row of vaults. (Photo taken in Iran by Bernard Gardi)

  **c** Laying the first slanting courses of bricks, supported by a wall as shown in **a**. (Photo taken in France by CRATerre)

  **d** A completed Nubian vault. (Photo of one of Hassan Fathy's buildings, taken in Egypt by Christine Bastin, 1980)

**7** Methods of constructing a dome in unbaked earth bricks without the use of centring:

  **a** Building a pendentive between arches. (Photo taken in France by CRATerre)

  **b** Building a squinch to support the dome. (Photo taken in Iran by Nader Khalili)

  **c** Completing the dome. (Photo taken in Iran by Nader Khalili)

  **d** Series of domes on the roof of a mosque in North Yemen. (Photo by Yvette Vincent-Alleaume, 1976)

**8** Constructing an earth vault reinforced with wood, near Tahoua, Niger. (Photo courtesy of the Musée de l'Homme, Paris)

**9** Interior of a 'Haoussa vault', made of earth reinforced with wood, in the Sultan's palace at Dosso, Niger. (Photo by Souhlal/Cartem)

**10** Town houses before (foreground) and after (background) completion at Sa'dah, North Yemen. The Yemenite tradition of angling the corners upwards for strength is clearly visible. (Photo by Véronique Dollfuss, 1976)

**11** Air-view of the town center at Séojane, Iran. The domes cover the main thoroughfares of the bazaar. (Photo by Georg Gerster/Rapho, 1975)

**12** Egyptian frieze depicting various stages in the preparation of unbaked earth bricks and their use in building. (Photo courtesy L. Christians)

**13** A 19th-century German depiction of the use of unbaked earth in traditional rural buildings. (Photo courtesy L. Christians)

**14** French illustration, dating from about 1860, showing different stages in preparing unbaked earth bricks. The view is of the outskirts of Reims, France, showing the railway and cathedral in the background. (Photo by Roger Roche)

**15** House in southwest Saudi Arabia. Rows of projecting flat stones embedded in the earth walls protect them from the region's infrequent but violent outbursts of rain. (Photo by Michael Earls, 1980)

**16** Coating an earth house with mud in the region of Santa Fe, New Mexico. (Photo by Russell Lee/Library of Congress, c. 1930)

**17** Annual ritual of coating the mosque with earth, in a village of the Bambara tribe in Mali. (Photo by Marli Shamir, 1970)

**18** Coating the flat roof of a house in the Dades region of Morocco. (Photo by Christian Lignon, 1981)

**19** Facing a wall with earth, in the Algerian Sahara. (Photo by Helfried Weyer, 1979)

1

2

# 7 Architecture for Rich and Poor

Building a home in unbaked earth in no way reflects on the social class of the owner. On the contrary, since earth is available to rich or poor alike shame has been completely irrelevant. Throughout history, indeed, the decision-makers and more privileged members of society have appreciated the special merits of unbaked earth, just as their less fortunate contemporaries profited from its cheapness. The large number of palaces built either partially or totally in unbaked earth by the world's rulers include the palace at Knossos in Crete (2000 BC), the palace of the Governors at Mari in Mesopotamia (1900 BC), the palace of Pharaoh Amenophis III at Aklet-Aton near Thebes (1350 BC), the remains of Raqchi in Peru (AD 1450), the el Baki palace in Marrakesh (AD 1578), the palaces of the Dalai Lama in Tibet and the Emir of Daura in Nigeria (AD 1780) and the palace of the Governors of Santa Fe, New Mexico (AD 1609). It is surely significant that some heads of state of our own time who came from modest rural origins have this in common with others born into the bourgeoisie: they have all lived in unbaked earth homes. Chairman Mao Tse-tung, for example, was born in an earth house in China (now a museum), just as President Ronald Reagan's Californian residence is constructed in adobe.

Earth architecture is indigenous to both rich and poor countries. But because it is more prevalent in the Third World than in the West, the governments of developing countries often despise their traditional building material as a symbol of the 'primitiveness' from which they are trying to escape. Instead they aspire to a more materialistic image of Western progress. Yet, at the same time, privileged citizens of the industrialized countries, in turn, are rediscovering the unique qualities of unbaked earth.

1 Rural dwellings in the High Atlas mountains, Morocco. (Photo by David Hicks, 1976)

2 Palace of the royal family at Riyadh, Saudi Arabia. (Photo by René Burri/Magnum)

3 Dining room of the Casa Estudillo, built in the 19th century at San Diego, California. (Photo by Christine Bastin, 1981)

4 House of the sheikh (village chieftain) of Bouadel, in the Rif region of Morocco. (Photo by Christian Lignon, 1981)

5 Courtyard of State in the emir's palace at Dansa in Nigeria. (Photo by Bruno Barbey/Magnum)

6 A 19th-century illustration of the palace of Ségou-Sikoro, on the River Niger in Mali.

7 A chateau of the 19th century, in the Saône valley near Lyons, France. (Photo by Patrice Doat and Hugo Houben)

8 Castle of the Glaoui, former feudal chieftains, built in the 19th century at Telouet in the High Atlas mountains of Morocco. (Photo by Anne Moreau, 1975)

9 The sultan's palace at Agadez, Niger. (Photo by Soulhal/Cartem)

10 Palace built at the beginning of the 20th century at Tarim in South Yemen, revealing both Indian and Indonesian influences. (Photo by Jean-François Breton and Christian Darles)

9

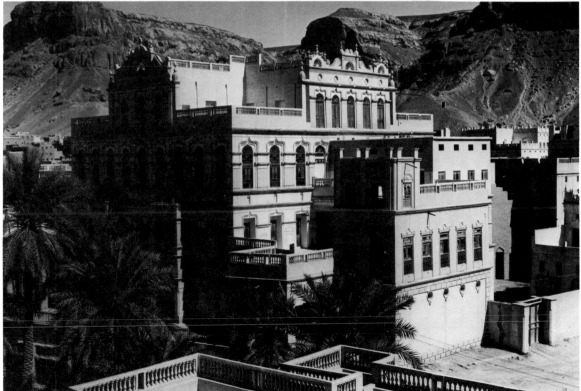

10

I

# 8 Urban Architecture in Unbaked Earth

Ever since men first congregated in urban communities they have used raw earth to construct both their dwellings and high ramparts to defend them. Archaeological remains testify to this practice among the most varied ancient communities. Later, from the Middle Ages onward, a magnificent heritage developed in the heart of towns as diverse as Marrakesh in Morocco, Bogotá in Colombia, Santa Fe in the USA and Granada in Spain, with the famous Alhambra, the former seat of government of the Arab princes. In modern times, recurrent revivals of earth construction have left their mark on towns. The highest modern building in raw earth in Europe, with seven floors, has stood since 1820 in the center of Weilburg (50 km north of Frankfurt) in West Germany. But it is around Santa Fe and Albuquerque that one finds the most significant products of the various 'adobe revivals' of this century. Marrakesh has the honour of possessing one of the most interesting social housing programmes in the Third World, consisting of a neighbourhood with over 3000 lodgings built in unbaked earth in 1965. In France the new town of l'Isle d'Abeau, between Lyons and Grenoble, is planned for 1982. This is Europe's first experimental urban project in raw earth, and is the brain-child of Jean Dethier and the Pompidou Center. It reconfirms traditional trust in the potential of building in this material, and aims to demonstrate its practicability for small towns, wherever local soil conditions are suitable.

5

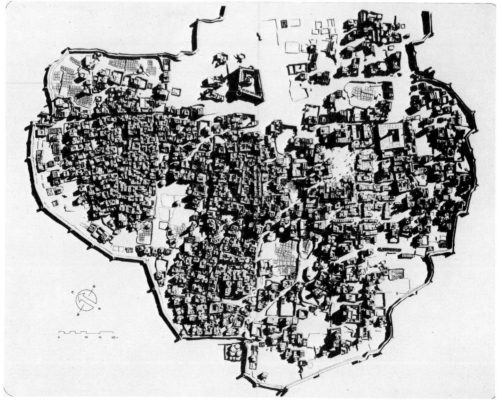

6

1 San'a, in North Yemen, has many five-storey houses. (Photo by Christian Monty, 1973)

2 A street in the suburbs of Lima, Peru. (Photo by Ovidio Oré, 1981)

3 Central square at Villa de Leyva, Colombia. (Photo by Ignacio Gomez Poulido, 1976)

4 Air-view of the center of Mopti in Mali, showing the great mosque (re-built in 1935) and the River Niger in the background. (Photo courtesy of the Musée de l'Homme, Paris, c. 1950)

5 The eight-storey houses of Shibam in the valley of Wadi Hadramaut, South Yemen (see ill. 7). Most of the buildings in this ancient city have been reconstructed during the second half of the 20th century. (Photo by Christian Darles and Jean-François Breton)

6 Plan of the city of Sa'dah in North Yemen, drawn by the architect Werner Dubach after an aerial survey conducted in 1973.

7 Air-view of Shibam in South Yemen (see photo 5). Background: the upper city with its 500 buildings; foreground: recent suburbs also built of unbaked earth. (Photo by Jean-François Breton and Christian Darles, 1978)

8 Air-view of the central district – the medina – of Marrakesh, Morocco. (Photo by Pierre Moreau)

9 Buildings of unbaked earth in the center of a Spanish town. (Photo by David Hicks)

10 Air-view of part of Lyons, France, built in pisé in the 19th century. (Photo courtesy of the Archives de la Ville de Lyon)

11 Street in San'a, North Yemen, where the buildings are of stone (usually the ground floor) and of unbaked earth. (Photo by André Biro, 1973)

12 Street in Santa Fe, New Mexico, a town founded by the Spanish. (Photo by Pierre Moreau)

13 Air-view of Tabrīz in Iran. (Photo by Georg Gerster/Rapho)

14 Air-view of Ta'izz, the second-largest city in North Yemen. In the foreground is the 19th-century Al-Ashrafiyah mosque. (Photo by Christian Monty, 1975)

# 9 Rural Architecture in Unbaked Earth

The rural areas that contain the vast majority of the world's earth buildings are far from being mostly in the Third World, for it should not be forgotten that these practices are familiar in the West: not only in the American Southwest but also in Europe. In France, 15 per cent of rural housing is still made of earth. In England, the West Country has its 'cob' or *pisé*, and East Anglia its 'clay lump'. From the south of Spain to the north of Denmark, many different forms and systems of construction have been developed, each one perfectly suited to the characteristics of its region. Sometimes earth buildings are grouped together, perhaps for purposes of defence, while at other times they are dispersed in a more individualistic manner. It is in rural communities that frequently very ancient traditions have been best conserved and saved from stultification.

Thus, for example, in the rugged pre-Saharan valleys of Morocco, such as the Dra and the Dades, we can still find villages which closely resemble the first urban complexes in which men congregated in the Near East, as well as recent buildings which reveal the influence of modern architecture. Rural earth architecture continues to evolve, harmoniously combining the lessons of the past with those for the future.

1 Rural fortified house – 'kasbah' – in the Dades valley, Morocco. (Photo by Anne Moreau)

2 Pueblo Indian village founded in New Mexico about 1250. (Photo courtesy of the Museum of New Mexico, Santa Fe, *c.* 1900; *see* pp. 55, ill. 15, taken in 1981)

3 Village in the Aurès mountains of Algeria. (Photo by David Hicks, 1976)

4 A thatched barn of *pisé*, in the Dauphiné region (Lake Paladru), France. (Photo by Patrice Doat and Hugo Houben, 1980)

5 A fortified rural house in the Wadi Khabb, North Yemen. (Photo by Pascal Maréchaux, 1980)

6 A farm built of *pisé* in Spain. (Photo by David Hicks, 1980)

7 Rural dwellings of the Gurunsi tribe in the village of Tiébélé, Upper Volta. (Photo by Bruno Français, 1981)

8 Rural dwelling in the Shansi region of China. (Photo by André Stevens, 1981)

9 Zoroastrian Sanctuary near Taft, in the region of Yazd in Iran. (Photo by Jean-François Cheval/Roger Viollet, 1978)

10 A fortified rural residence – 'kasbah' – in the Dades region of Morocco. (Photo by Karl-Heinz Streidter, 1969)

9

10

# 10 Ornamentation

The intense pleasure which traditional civilizations derive from manipulating ornamentation and conveying vital forces in potent signs, is expressed in the artistic attention lavished on their earth architecture. Engraved on the walls or applied in relief, it is in turn abstract, gestural, geometric, symbolic and figurative. Some of these techniques of earth building are relatively easy to master, enabling the inhabitants – either partially or entirely – to construct their homes themselves.

Their walls are often protected by coatings consisting mainly of raw earth, and these are traditionally renewed each year in the course of a ritual that follows the rainy season. The façades thus change annually and can vary infinitely as each individual expresses his creative impulses in the visual, tactile and sensual richness of the walls.

Earth construction is thus fused with artistic creation, for the ornamentation is as organically linked to the walls as it is to the society that produces it.

2

6

7

**1** House built in 1947 in the town of Zinder, Niger. (Photo by Michel Renaudeau, 1970)

**2** Pillar in the form of a fetish, standing in the exterior gallery of a village-chief's house, Ivory Coast. (Photo by François-Xavier Bouchart, 1977)

**3** Decorating the earth walls of houses in Oualata, Mauritania. (Photo courtesy of the Musée Ethnographique, Neuchâtel)

**4** Detail of earth tracery at the base of the dome of a mosque at Djibla, North Yemen. (Photo by Christian Monty, 1975)

**5** Decorating the earth walls at Zinder, Niger. (Photo by R. Gardi)

**6** A fetish, worked in relief on the wall of a house of the Sénoufo tribe, on the Ivory Coast. (Photo by François-Xavier Bouchart)

**7** An 18th-century Baroque church in Peru. (Photo by Ovidio Oré, 1981)

**8** Façade of a traditional Bozo house near Mopti in Mali. (Photo by Sergio Domian, 1981)

**9** Upper floors of a kasbah (fortified house) near El Kelaa des Mgouna, in the Dades valley, Morocco. (Photo by Christian Lignon, 1981)

**10** Walls at the entrance to a house of the Songhaï tribe in the Upper Volta. (Photo by Bruno Français, 1980)

**11** An incised ornamental earth wall, restored on the site of Chan-Chan, 13th-century capital of the Chimú civilization in Peru. (Photo by Ovidio Oré)

**12** Detail of the restored walls at Chan-Chan. (Photo by D. Lavallée)

**13** Figures in relief adorn panels on the walls of the royal palace at Abomey, Dahomey. (Photo courtesy of the Musée Ethnographique, Neuchâtel, c. 1979)

**14** Traditional ornamentation in a courtyard at Oualata, Mauritania. (Photo courtesy of the Musée Ethnographique, Neuchâtel, 1975)

**15** Decorated façade in Al Juba, North Yemen. (Photo by Pascal Maréchaux, 1980)

**16** The emir in front of the palace at Zaria, Nigeria. (Photo by François-Xavier Bouchart)

13

# 11  Sensuality

Building in earth seems to provoke a particularly physical creative urge in its craftsmen. The fertility of soil itself perhaps inspires pleasure by naturally forming voluptuous curves which the maker caresses as he works. Architecture is therefore the expression of profound impulses as well as producing images of physical and 'earthy' pleasure. This immediacy and urgency invests domestic and communal spaces with a powerful erotic dimension, radiant with the joy of creation.

A fine example is in Mali, where earth architecture surpasses the technical constraints of building, reflecting a delight in working this most basic raw material. Men and women translate this creative drive into a language which is all the more vital and elemental since it is perpetually in a state of flux and rebirth: the forms of sculptural vocabulary are remodelled, reinterpreted and revitalized each year after the rainy season in a festive ritual. This mode of production involves a direct relationship with the material since it requires neither the use of complex instruments nor academic or technological knowledge. Instead, it demands only the desire of each 'architect' to participate in the traditions of the society and their eternal renewal, in harmony with the cultural heritage and the spirit of place.

2

4

5

# 12 The Sky's the Limit

Could the first-ever skyscraper have been built of unbaked earth? For that was undoubtedly the material out of which the 'Tower of Babel' was constructed in the 7th century BC in Babylon. Captain Robert Mignan recorded in 1829 that: 'The remains of the Tower of Babel [are] composed of kiln-burnt and sun-dried bricks, rising irregularly to the height of 139 feet'. It is estimated that its seventh level once topped a height of 90 meters, and a number of other towns in ancient Mesopotamia contained vast, tiered towers or 'ziggurats', which were frequently about 40 ot 50 meters high. These building traditions have been handed down through many centuries, and people still continue to use raw earth for the construction of towering edifices.

Castles ('kasbahs') and fortified villages ('ksars') of the pre-Saharan valleys of Morocco, often rise to four storeys, as do villages of North American Indians such as that at Taos. The lofty minarets of mosques in Africa and the Middle East seem to defy gravity. But the city of Shibam in South Yemen is surely more amazing than all of these, and is often nicknamed 'Manhattan of the Desert' because its 500 buildings resemble a forest of skyscrapers, many of them rising to eight levels and standing 30 meters high. Although this building technique is part of a very ancient tradition in the Yemen, half the buildings in Shibam have been erected during this century, proving that the custom thrives and can be readily adapted to suit the needs of contemporary city life.

1 A 30 m-high minaret crowns the prayer-courtyard of the great mosque at Agadez, Niger, founded around 1500 and rebuilt *c.* 1844. (Photo by Jacques Evrard, 1970)

2 Tower in the ramparts of Rbat El Ajar, a ksar in the Dra valley, Morocco. (Photo by Christian Lignon, 1981)

3 Towers at the gateway of the ksar of Igoulmime, near Goulmina, in the Gheris valley, Morocco. (Photo by Christian Lignon, 1981)

4 Minaret at Hazrat Sale, Afghanistan. (Photo by Roland Michaud/Rapho, 1976)

5 Minaret of the Al Mikhdar mosque at Tarim, South Yemen, seems to defy gravity. (Photo by Jean-François Breton and Christian Darles, 1979)

6 Minaret at Moka, North Yemen. (Photo by André Biro, 1978)

7 Façade of the mosque at Koro, Mali. (Photo by Sylviane and Pierre Leprun, 1981)

8 Recent house containing five storeys, in the town of Shibam, South Yemen. (Photo by Christian Darles and Jean-François Breton, 1977)

5

6

# 13 The Grandeur of Earth Buildings

Unbaked earth constructions can be not only very high, but also on a scale suitable for the communal activities of villages and cities. Although the majority are individual homes, many 'houses of God' are also built of earth, and some achieve monumental dimensions. These include chapels, churches, monasteries and even cathedrals such as that in Lima, Peru. In the USA, a tradition of vast naves in unbaked earth was established in the 18th century following the construction of the Mission San Xavier del Bac at Tucson, Arizona. The Cristo Rey Church in Santa Fe, the largest modern building in unbaked earth in America, proves that this tradition has flourished up to the present day. The great mosque at Mopti in Mali, erected in 1935, is probably the largest and most imposing public building constructed in Africa in unbaked earth during this century, and its builders used only traditional building techniques in constructing this vast and majestic edifice: as such, it constitutes a monumental challenge to modern technology.

1  An 18th-century Baroque church in Peru. (Photo by Ovidio Oré, 1981)

2  Mausoleum in the village of Ghuraf in the Wadi Hadramaut region of South Yemen. (Photo by Jean-François Breton and Christian Darles, 1978)

3  Interior of the church of San Miguel, built by the Spanish in New Mexico. (Photo by Malcolm Lubliner, 1980)

4  Ramparts of the town of Bam in Iran. (Photo by Bruno Barbey/Magnum, 1978)

5  Church of San Xavier del Bac, founded c. 1783 near Tucson, Arizona. (Photo by Jacques Evrard and Christine Bastin, 1981)

6  Friday prayers at the great mosque of Mopti in Mali, rebuilt 1935. (Photo by Georg Gerster/Rapho, 1978)

4

5

# 14  Interiors and Harmony

One senses a wonderfully harmonious atmosphere in earth houses. This is partly because the same material is used throughout the building, and partly because of the nature of the spaces formed, and the architectural rhythms that are dictated by the nature of unbaked earth.

A physical and spiritual awareness and invigorating sensuality often emanate from these interiors, be they modest or princely. Since the same material is used for everything, sometimes even the furniture, the interiors are artistic environments linked to the pace of daily life: they are living sculptures, inhabited by men and expressing their ornamental skills. This creative momentum takes on a different character in mosques, for there the space becomes a forest of massive pillars which span the area of prayer and lend it an uncanny emotional force.

But the strength of earth architecture is not only spiritual; it is also physically comfortable. Earth buildings are cool in summer and warm in winter, for by their very nature the thick earth walls provide protection against extremes of climate outside, creating natural thermal regulation. This ensures very considerable savings in energy. The revival of earth architecture has enabled us to rediscover this ancient empirical knowledge, inherited from countless generations over the centuries.

3

1  Interior of the mosque at Zaria, Nigeria. Photo taken in 1970 by Allan Leary, before 'modernizations' destroyed the character of the place.

2  View into the roof of a house at Tiflet (Imergham), Morocco. (Photo by David Hicks, 1969)

3  Interior of a rural house, built 1976 in the village of Al Jubayriah, North Yemen. (Photo by Werner Dubach, 1976)

4  Interior of a house of the Haoussa tribe in Niger. The walls and furniture are entirely of earth. (Photo by Sylviane Leprun)

5  Sitting-room of a house at Santa Fe, New Mexico. (Photo courtesy of the Museum of New Mexico)

6  Interior of a peasant home at Younine, in the Beqa'a region of Lebanon. (Photo by Jacques Liger-Bellair, 1972)

7  Audience chamber of a notable's house, at Thula, North Yemen. (Photo by André Biro, 1978)

8  Prayer hall of the mosque of Goulmina, in the Gheris valley, Morocco. (Photo by Karl-Heinz Striedter, 1970)

9  Aisle of the prayer hall in the great mosque at Djenne, Mali, reconstructed 1905. The pillars are about 15 m high. (Photo by Samir El Sadi, 1978)

10  Reception room – 'mafrejd' – in a notable's house in the town of Buraydah, in central Saudi Arabia. (Photo by Christian Monty, 1973)

11  Interior of a convent built in the 18th century at Popayan, Colombia. (Photo by Ignacio Gomez Pulido, 1979)

12  Reception room of a middle-class home in southwest Saudi Arabia. (Photo by Michael Earls, 1980)

# 15 Ruins, Restorations and Ruses

Over one-third of the world's population lives in earth houses, and this traditional construction method continues to thrive in most of the Third World. For modern Western technology has failed, both financially and socially, to satisfy the increasing demand for cheap housing. In countries recently enriched by oil, these traditions have tended suddenly to disappear as happened in Europe during the 1930s and 1950s. They are nowadays – as then – replaced by architectural forms and technologies which are considered to be indicative of social advancement, even though they are notoriously ill-adapted to local climatic conditions.

But the tide is changing, and since 1972 in the American Southwest groups of enthusiasts have brought about a revival of earth architecture for both communal and domestic uses. We are now, therefore, witnessing a series of simultaneous but discordant phenomena: in some regions of the world the architectural heritage is being abandoned or dying out, while in other countries earth buildings are now prized as important examples of universal wisdom, and are listed, restored and protected. In addition, universities, academies and international institutions are attempting to forge a productive link between traditions and modernity. However, this enthusiasm sometimes leads to the wildest parodies, committed by those hoping for quick profits. Some are not constructed in unbaked earth at all, and are perversions that betray the very spirit and nature of earth architecture which, thanks to popular traditions, has always been able to suit an entire spectrum of differing circumstances.

1 Abandoned ksar in the Ziz valley, Morocco. (Photo by Karl-Heinz Striedter, 1970)

2 Ksar of Tamezmoute in the Dra valley, Morocco. Background: the redundant feudal castle; foreground: houses restored and modernized as part of a United Nations development programme. (Photo by Karl-Heinz Striedter)

3 Remains of the Ziggurat of Agar-Guf, built under Kuzigalzu I (1390–1379 BC) in Iran. Restoration began in 1942. (Photo by André Stevens, 1978)

4 Remains of the 'El Badi' palace, built in Marrakesh, Morocco, by King Ahmed el Mansour in 1578. (Photo provided by A. Paccard)

5 An earth-built mosque abandoned in favour of a new one of cement, at Bouna on the Ivory Coast. (Photo by François-Xavier Bouchart)

6 Ksar of Tissergate, in the Dra valley, Morocco, restored and modernized in 1969 by the local community as part of a rehabilitation programme supported by the United Nations. (Photo by Christian Lignon, 1981)

7 Stupa (or funerary monument), built in the 12th century in the city of Qotcho (Turfan region), China, recently restored. (Photo by André Stevens)

8 Reconstructed temple of Emach at Babylon, Iraq. (Photo by André Stevens, 1981; see p. 22)

9 Mosque for Muslim Senegalese troops of the French colonial army. Constructed about 1930 at the barracks near Fréjus, France, it is a travesty of the earth mosques in Mali for it is built entirely out of cement. (Photo by François-Xavier Bouchart, 1980)

10 Luxury hotel built in central Santa Fe, New Mexico, 1980. Using the architectural forms and rhythms of Indian villages in New Mexico such as the Taos Pueblo (see p. 55, ill. 15), this building is a commercial parody of the regional culture, being constructed out of reinforced concrete. (Photo by Pierre Moreau)

# 16 The Modernity of Traditions

As we approach the end of our flying visit to the earth architecture of about 30 countries, we can see that this form of building is far from being a thing of the past. Not only do a third of our contemporaries still live in earth buildings, but traditional methods show every sign of being the most effective and realistic way we shall discover of resolving current world-wide problems of housing. We have now shown that the barrier between tradition and modernity in this domain is artificial, and that to break it down we must undo the work of those who, half a century ago, sought to erase our past and plunge us into an era of amnesia and cultural intolerance: who imposed on us their stereotyped schemes for 'progress at any price' claiming they were suitable anywhere and everywhere, and whom we have shown to be no less than the cultural imperialists of the 'International Style'.

But the solution is not to gaze nostalgically at traditions and to claim they can be adopted just as we find them. Cultural traditions are not frozen in time; they are constantly reviewed, reinterpreted and renewed in order to create a vital link between history and locale. Certain architects of the modern era have tried to forge this connection, in direct response to the needs of their own, and our, time. It is these pioneers whom we shall now consider, in order to complete this summary of traditions and to see how earth construction is being called to a new destiny.

ECOLE D'ARCHITECTURE RURALE

3  4

**1** Villa based on traditional styles, built *c*. 1930 at Adrar in the Algerian Sahara. (Photo by Karl-Heinz Striedter, 1975)

**2** Watercolour design by the architect Hassan Fathy, for a villa built in Egypt *c*. 1960. (Photo by Christine Bastin)

**3** School of Rural Architecture, designed by François Cointeraux in about 1789. This is the earliest known attempt to employ *pisé* as a modern constructional material. It has *trompe-l'oeil* painting on the façade. (Photo by Jacques Evrard)

**4** Town house built in 1959 at Agadez in Niger. It is an excellent illustration of the new tendency in some parts of Africa to adapt traditional techniques to modern needs. (Photo by Jacques Evrard, 1970)

**5** The great mosque of Mopti in Mali, rebuilt in 1935. (Photo by René Gardi)

**6** A 19th-century house in colonial style in central Santa Fe, New Mexico. Except for the wooden pergola at the front it is of unbaked earth. (Photo by Pierre Moreau)

**7** Houses built about 1970 at Tamezmoute in the Dra valley, Morocco. (Photo by Christian Lignon, 1981)

# Architecture in Earth: New Prospects, New Projects

The first attempts to modernize and even industrialize the use of unbaked earth are far from recent, having taken place two centuries ago in the late 18th century. Then, at the dawn of the modern era, the first industrialized societies were facing problems not unlike our own. It has remained characteristic that periods of intense research into earth architecture have successively coincided with great economic crises.

This chain of research and experiment began in France shortly before the Revolution, when, in 1772, Goiffon published *L'Art du maçon piseur* ('The art of the *pisé* builder'), the first known book entirely devoted to the subject. François Cointeraux (1740–1830) can claim, however, to be the first architect of modern times to combine research and experimentation with the construction of modern buildings in unbaked earth. His entire career was devoted to the modernization of techniques of *pisé de terre*, or rammed earth, which he viewed as one of the solutions to the economic and social crisis plaguing his country at the time. He proposed modifying traditional methods, which would then be suitable for all types of housing, for public buildings, for urban manufactories and for rural constructions.

Even before his death, Cointeraux's ideas had become known in several countries, and many disciples had taken up his cause: Holland and Barber in England, Gilman and Johnson in the USA, and Gilly, Sachs, Conradi, Engel and Wimpf in Germany. Other advocates, whose names are unknown, carried his doctrines to Scandinavia, Australia and Italy where his prolific writings were translated and published.

The 20th century, similarly, has produced theoreticians and practicians of earth architecture mostly at times when industrial society was experiencing serious economic crises, or had to embark upon large-scale rebuilding programmes after wars had devastated housing and destroyed the factories that produced building materials. Such was the case in Europe following the First World War, when the works of Clough Williams-Ellis and Karl and Inez Ellington led to schemes in various countries. Such too was the case in the USA when the economic crisis of the 1930s saw the blossoming of laboratory research and many experimental projects of earth building. This work encouraged a domestic 'Adobe Revival', a number of regional development schemes and considerable military use of the material.

During the Second World War, both the Allies and the Axis Powers sought to conserve their energy and material resources by using unbaked earth for various types of construction. Architects as varied and well-known as Le Corbusier in France, Albert Speer in Germany and Frank Lloyd Wright in America, all helped to promote construction in earth between 1940 and 1945.

This work expanded after the war, when entire towns and villages had been destroyed. Reconstruction programmes made use of unbaked earth in England, France, West Germany and, above all, East Germany, where the trend lasted right through until the 1960s. East Germany also exported its expertise in this field to other socialist countries in economic difficulties, such as North Korea.

The post-war world also saw the birth of independence movements in European colonies, and the rejection of Western ways. Their search for cultural identity was perhaps most eloquently voiced by the Egyptian architect Hassan Fathy, who vigorously opposed the importation of Western models and promoted the revival and modernization of historical and popular traditions of building in unbaked earth. His experimental village 'New Gourna' became a cultural symbol, while Fathy himself was regarded as a guru by young architects in the Third World reluctant to accept Western stereotypes.

The People's Republic of China, faced with the political and economic need to rely only on its own resources, built everything from dams to commune centers in raw earth during the 1950s and 1960s. Even the United Nations, during the critical years of the 1950s, when many colonies were granted independence, encouraged construction in raw earth in 'economically underdeveloped countries'.

The 1950s and 1960s saw the establishment of many other raw-earth building schemes, both urban and rural, situated in Latin America, Africa and the Middle East, mostly in response to the economic crisis, the rural exodus and the demographic explosion.

When the energy crisis struck Western as well as Third World oil importers in 1973, energy conservation became an almost obsessional leitmotif for nations hoping to safeguard their economic and political independence. At the same time, the West suffered a serious economic recession, large-scale unemployment – a total of 20 million in the EEC and the USA in 1982 – and an ecological crisis of conscience. In this uncertain world, with the foundations of industrialized society well and truly shaken, it is easy to comprehend the recent resurgence of interest in architecture in unbaked earth. The late 1970s and early 1980s are witnessing the simultaneous appearance on all five continents of a lively interest among architects, engineers, governments and potential users, in the modernization and expansion of this time-honoured practice. Never before have so many modern buildings been constructed in unbaked earth in so short a time and in so many different countries. Never before has the feasibility of construction in unbaked earth been demonstrated more effectively or more convincingly.

## Pioneers in Europe During the 18th and 19th Centuries

*Previous pages* Part of 'La Luz', the suburb designed by Antoine Predock in 1974 on the outskirts of Albuquerque, New Mexico. (Photo by Jacques Evrard and Christine Bastin, 1981; *see* pp. 178–81)

**1** Milton Abbas, a village built in Dorset in 1773 on the initiative of the Earl of Dorchester, who appears to have entrusted the design to William Chambers and Capability Brown. (Photo by Gillian Darley, 1978)

**2** A 6-storey building constructed during the 19th century at Weilburg in Germany by the architect Wimpf, under the influence of the works of François Cointeraux. It survives in perfect condition. (Photo courtesy of CRATerre)

**3** Title page of the *School of Rural Architecture*, published by François Cointeraux in Paris, 1790. It is subtitled: 'Lessons on building strong and durable houses, to the height of several storeys, out of nothing but earth'. He worked mainly between 1789 and 1815.

**4** The 19th-century German architect Wimpf built a vast factory in *pisé* at Weilburg, directly inspired by the works of François Cointeraux, and in particular by his project of 1790 for a manufactory (*see* ill. 6). (Photo courtesy of CRATerre)

**5** Houses designed after the French Revolution of 1789 for members of different social classes. This double illustration is the best known of François Cointeraux's designs for unbaked earth architecture. The captions suggest a single model, to be altered according to the needs of the user: (*left*) 'A decorated house in earth or *pisé*', and (*right*) 'The same house direct from the worker's hands'.

**6** Plan and elevation of a manufactory to be built in *pisé*, designed by François Cointeraux in 1790.

ÉCOLE
D'ARCHITECTURE RURALE,
*ou*
LEÇONS.

Par lesquelles on apprendra soi-même à bâtir solidement les maisons de plusieurs étages avec la terre seule, ou autres matériaux les plus communs et du plus vil prix.

OUVRAGE DÉDIÉ AUX FRANÇAIS,

*Par* François Cointeraux, *ancien Estimateur d'immeubles de la campagne, ou ancien Expert et Arpenteur Juré, Maître Maçon, Agriculteur, et Architecte.*

A PARIS,
Chez l'Auteur, grande rue Verte, fauxbourg Saint-Honoré, N°. 15; ou dans son atelier, même fauxbourg, au Colisée, près des Tuileries.
Et chez les principaux Libraires de Paris et des provinces.

Mars 1790.

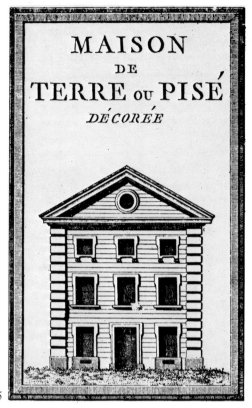

MAISON
DE
TERRE ou PISÉ
DÉCORÉE

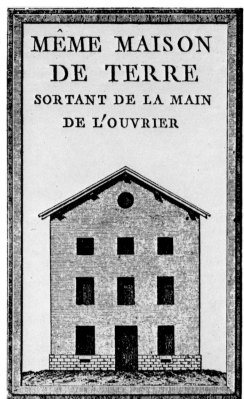

MÊME MAISON
DE TERRE
SORTANT DE LA MAIN
DE L'OUVRIER

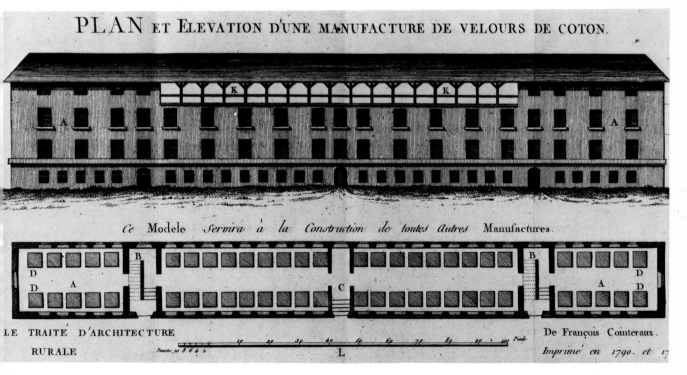

PLAN ET ÉLÉVATION D'UNE MANUFACTURE DE VELOURS DE COTON.

Ce Modele servira à la Construction de toutes autres Manufactures.

LE TRAITÉ D'ARCHITECTURE
RURALE

De François Cointeraux.

Imprimé en 1790. et 17

**The First Suburban Villas
and Country Houses
in Europe and the USA**

**1** Cottage at Budleigh Salterton, Devon, by Ernest Gimson, *c.* 1920. (Photo by Christian Besnard)

**2** Suburban house built in Germany *c.* 1920. (Photo by L. Christians)

**3** A 19th-century house in southwest USA. (Photo courtesy of the Museum of New Mexico, Santa Fe)

**4** Design for a country house by the 18th-century French architect Claude Nicolas Ledoux. (Photo by Christian Besnard)

**5** House near Zurich, Switzerland, built in about 1885. (Photo by Christian Besnard)

**6** The elaborately Victorian 'Castle Huning', built in 1883 in Albuquerque, New Mexico. (Photo courtesy of the Albuquerque Art Museum)

**7** A villa built in Norway about 1910. (Photo by Christian Besnard)

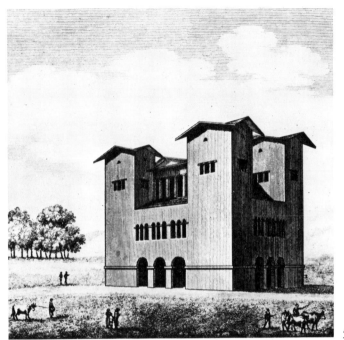

5

6

7

## Modern Architecture in Unbaked Earth: Le Corbusier, Frank Lloyd Wright and Schindler

**1** Design for a villa at El Paso, Texas, 1942, by Frank Lloyd Wright (1869–1959). He was working in adobe at the same period. (Photo courtesy of the Frank Lloyd Wright Foundation)

**2** Design for a country home at Taos, New Mexico, by the Austrian architect Rudolph Schindler (1887–1953). It dates from 1915 while he was on a trip to New Mexico. He was highly impressed by the variety of architectural traditions in the American Southwest. (Photo by Christian Besnard)

**3** Part of a series of drawings by Le Corbusier in 1940, which appeared in *Les Murondins* (1941), dedicated to 'my friends, the youth of France'. (Documents courtesy of the Fondation Le Corbusier)

A COUNTRY HOME IN ADOBE CONSTR FOR DR T P MARTIN TAOS NEW MEXICO R M SCHINDLER ARCH

LE CORBUSIER

# LES **M**AISONS "**M**URONDINS"
## PETIT CADEAU A MES AMIS, LES JEUNES DE FRANCE

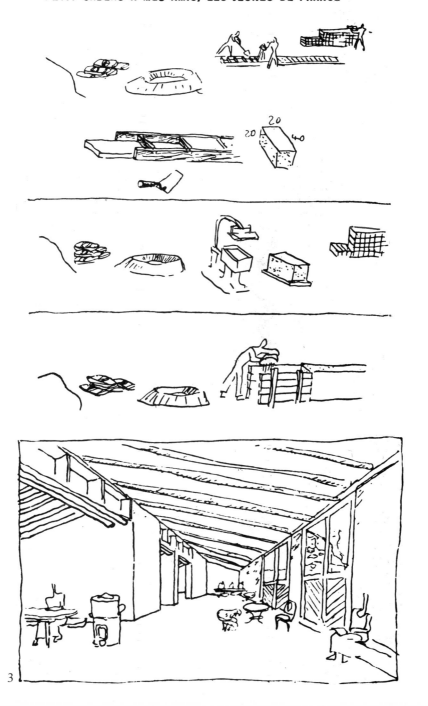

## New Technology in the Third World and the USA

**1,2** Experimental urban housing, built in 1968 at Ouarzazate, Morocco, by the French engineer Alain Masson and the Belgian architect Jean Hensens. (Photos by Alain Masson)

**3** Experimental housing built in 1972 at Zeralda, Algeria, by a Franco-Belgian team of architects and engineers: Hugo Houben, Paul Pedrotti and Dirk Belmans. (Photo by Paul Pedrotti, 1973)

**4,5** Nader Khalili is seeking to revive traditional methods of building in unbaked earth in Iran, where they were scorned during the rule of the Shah in favour of imported Western models and materials. Since 1980 he has directed several experimental schemes of restoration and construction. Once the buildings are completed, he vitrifies the interiors with huge fires. By using the natural elements of earth, air, fire and water, his architecture has gained a quasi-mystical character in the eyes of the religious leaders of the Islamic revolution. (Photo by Nader Khalili)

**6** Manual press for adobe brickmaking, designed and patented in 1957 by Paul Ramirez in Colombia on behalf of the CINVA housing association. This was the first machine of its kind, producing blocks in large quantities, and of a quality which is far more resistant than those moulded by hand. (Photo taken in Mali by Jean-Claude Pivin, 1981)

**7** Stabilized earth bricks, made in a small semi-industrial production plant in New Mexico. (Photo by Jacques Evrard)

5

7

## A Mosque by an Egyptian Architect in the USA, 1981

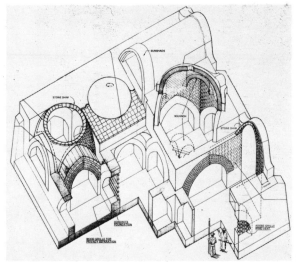

1

**1** Axonometric drawing of the mosque built in 1981 by the Egyptian architect Hassan Fathy in Abiquiu, New Mexico (*see* p. 157). (Drawing provided by the American review, *Adobe Today*)

**2, 3** Mosque built in Abiquiu, New Mexico, by Hassan Fathy in 1981. Its construction was accompanied by training courses for American architects in recently revived traditional building methods. These include the 'Nubian vault' (*see* p. 60) and the dome (*see* p. 61) which are now being constructed in Egypt out of unbaked earth without centring. This has made a deep impression on Americans, who did not expect to become the beneficiaries of 'technical and cultural assistance' from the Third World. (Photos by Jacques Evrard and Christine Bastin, 1981)

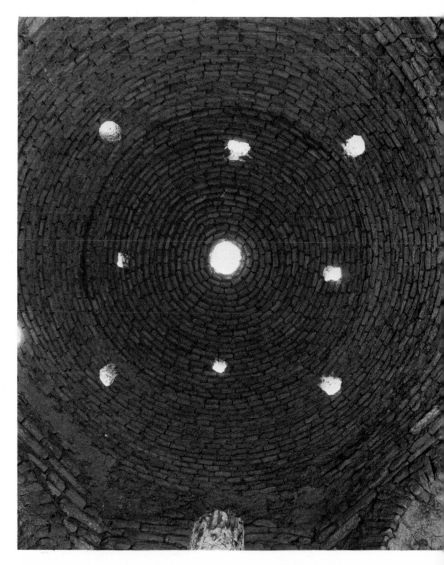

**Medical Center at Mopti in Mali**

1

**1, 2** Medical center built in 1976 at Mopti in Mali, between the great mosque (rebuilt in 1935) and the River Niger. It is the work of the French architect André Ravereau and a Belgian colleague Philippe Lauwers, who undertook this scheme for the Malian Ministry of Planning, under the aegis of the European Development Fund. This branch of the European Economic Community has been trying for some time, primarily at the instigation of its architectural advisor Marc Wolf, to promote technologies in the Third World which are adapted to the characteristics of each region. This example won, in 1980, one of the ten Aga Khan Awards, set up to encourage high architectural standards and a new synthesis between architectural tradition and modernity in Muslim countries. (Photos by Sylviane Leprun in 1981 and Emmanuelle Roche in 1979)

2

## Two Hospitals in Africa

**1** Model of the extension of the hospital of Kaédi, planned for construction in 1982 under the Yugoslav architect Dusan Stanimirovic, a member of the French group 'Ciet-Inter-G', with the aid of the European Development Fund (*see* pp. 158–9). (Photo by Beaugeaud, 1980)

**2–6** Regional hospital at Adrar in the Algerian Sahara, built in 1942 by the French architect Michel Luyckx, a student and disciple of Auguste Perret. This represents the first successful synthesis in the 20th century between traditional techniques and modern architecture without whimsey. After 40 years of use, it remains effective and reliable, and well atuned to climatic conditions. Michel Luyckx was clearly an important pioneer.

**3, 5** Views of the hospital under construction; **6** Water-tower covered in unbaked earth to prevent overheating; **2** Façade of the hospital chapel; **4** Model of the entire hospital complex. (Photos by Michel Luyckx, 1944 and 1946)

(*Below*) Plan of the hospital complex, with the cross-shaped water-tower in the center.

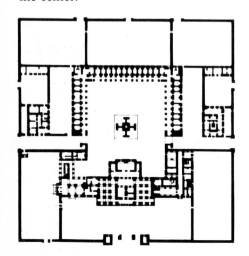

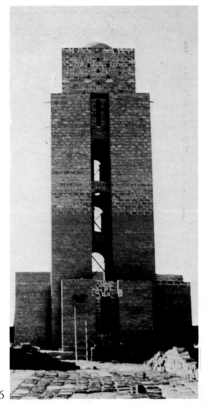

6

# Three Hotels in Africa and the USA

**1, 4** Sitting room and a bedroom of the 'Sagebrush Inn', built about 1930 at Ranchos de Taos, New Mexico. Its welcoming architecture has assured its fame and commercial success. (Photos by Jacques Evrard, 1981)

**2** 'Salt Lick Game Lodge', in the Tsavo National Park, 150 km from Mombassa, Kenya. (Photo by Bernard Mailles, 1980)

**3** 'Hôtel de l'oasis rouge' (Red Oasis Hotel), built about 1930 in the new town of Timimoun in the Algerian Sahara. (Photo by Anne Rochette, 1981)

## Training Center in Senegal

## Training Project for Builders in Mauritania

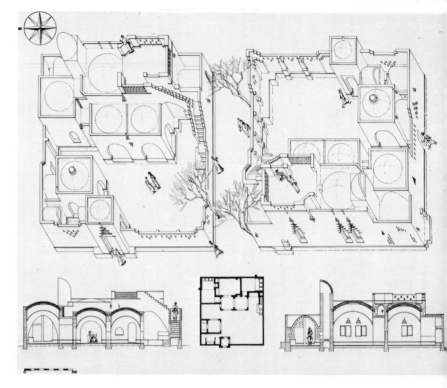

**1** Axonometric views, plan and sections of a prototype of urban housing, built in 1979 at Rosso, Mauritania, by the French architect Serge Theunynck, a member of the international ADAUA group ('Workshop for the Development of African Architecture and Urbanism'). This was used for training local workers to build walls, vaults and domes with unbaked earth bricks, so that knowledge of these processes might encourage an 'owner-builder' approach to popular housing. (Documents redrawn by Dominique Pidance and Alain Le Balh, 1981)

**2–4** Buildings of the Agricultural Training Center, built in 1977 by the Belgian architect Oswald Dellicour under the aegis of UNESCO and on behalf of the Ministry of Education at Nianing in Senegal. They were constructed out of earth from the site on which they stand. In 1980 this project received an Aga Khan Award (*see also* pp. 158–9), which encourages the adaptation of architecture to different localities. (Photos by Oswald Dellicour, 1979)

**Three Cultural Institutions
in Mali and the USA**

**1–3** Preliminary sketch, work in progress and the completed building of the Beaux-Arts Museum, a department of the Museum of New Mexico built in 1917 in the center of Santa Fe by the American architects Rapp and Rapp. Directly inspired by the historic convent and church of Acoma, this museum played an important role in stimulating the 'Santa Fe revival style', whose nostalgic formalism today seems such an aesthetic parody. Although this building engendered a reevaluation of architecture in unbaked earth, it is in fact constructed out of fired bricks covered in cement. (Photos courtesy of the Museum of New Mexico, 1917 and 1920)

**4** National Museum of Mali, opened at Bamako in 1981 and designed by the French architect Jean-Claude Pivin, helped by the museum designer Pierre Gaudibert. (Photo by Jean-Claude Pivin, 1981)

**5** Annexe of the Beaux-Arts Museum at Santa Fe, New Mexico: the History Library. (Photo by Pierre Moreau, 1980)

# Four Research Centers
# in Africa and Europe

**1** Façade of the regional crafts center built in 1979 at Er Rachidia, Morocco, by the French architect Jean-Paul Ichter. Different construction techniques are skilfully combined: stone foundations, supporting walls of *pisé*, and spaces filled with traditional ornamental screens of unbaked earth bricks. The flat roof of reinforced concrete rests on beams which project beyond the walls. (Photo by Anne Moreau, 1980)

**2–5** Project entered for a competition organized in 1981 for a Technological Research Center to be constructed in unbaked earth at the architectural school of Marseille-Luminy in France. It was designed by the French architects Serge Theunynck (*see* p. 164), Nicolas Widmer, Paul Wagner, Luc Gauthier and the thermal engineer Daniel Favre. (Plans and drawings by the architects)

**6** Project for the research center of the American archaeological mission at Karnak in Egypt, designed 1976–8 by the Californian architect George Homsey of the firm of Esherick, Homsey, Dodge and Davis. In 1979 this project received the annual Design Award from the American architectural review, *Progressive Architecture*. (Axonometric drawing by Jerry Kuriyama)

**7** Research center of the French archaeological mission at Karnak, Egypt, built mainly by the French architect, Jacques Vérité. (Photo by Jacques Evrard)

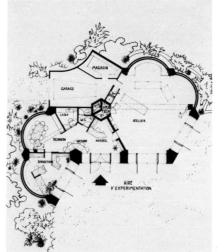

2

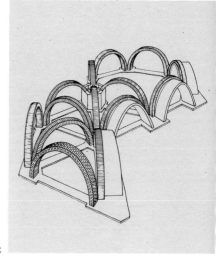

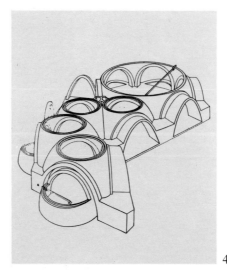

4

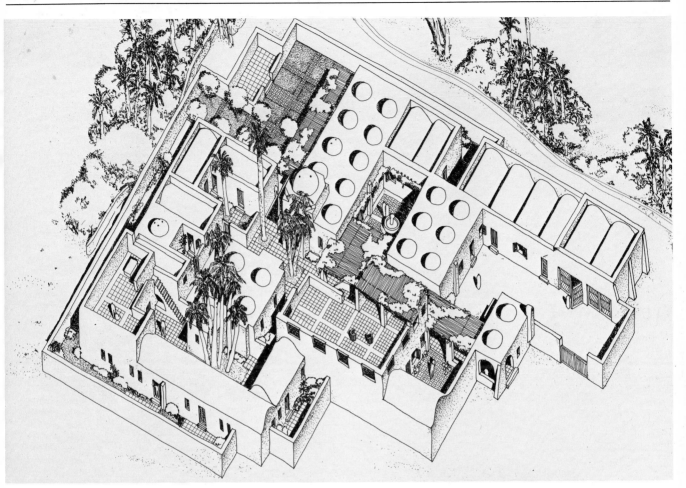

**Two Chapels, a Church
and a Monastery in the USA**

1

2

**1,5** Interior and exterior of the 'Cristo Rey' church, designed in 1940 by the American architect John Gaw Meem at Santa Fe, New Mexico. This is the largest modern public building constructed in raw earth in the USA. Its 180,000 adobe bricks were made at the site. (Photo by Christine Bastin, 1981)

**2** Chapel built *c.* 1930 on the campus of the University of New Mexico, Albuquerque. (Photo by Anne Moreau, 1979)

**3** Chapel built at Nambe Pueblo, New Mexico, *c.* 1979. (Photo by Jacques Evrard, 1981)

**4** Monastery built *c.* 1976 in New Mexico, after the plans of George Yakashima. This example of recent monumental architecture constructed out of raw earth avoids purely regional traditions and seeks more contemporary forms of expression. (Photo by Mark Chalom, 1978)

3

## Gourna: a New Village in Egypt

1 The Egyptian architect Hassan Fathy, photographed with his cat at his home in Cairo, by Jacques Evrard in 1980.

2 Plan of the village of New Gourna, built by Hassan Fathy in Egypt from 1946. White areas show the possible layout of grouped housing (*see* ill. 3); black spaces in the center of the village are reserved for public buildings. (Plan by Hassan Fathy)

3 Exterior of a house in New Gourna, Egypt (*see* ill. 2), built by Hassan Fathy. (Photo by Jacques Evrard, 1980)

4 Plans and façades of groups of dwellings designed by Hassan Fathy, drawn about 1950 for New Gourna. (Drawing by Hassan Fathy)

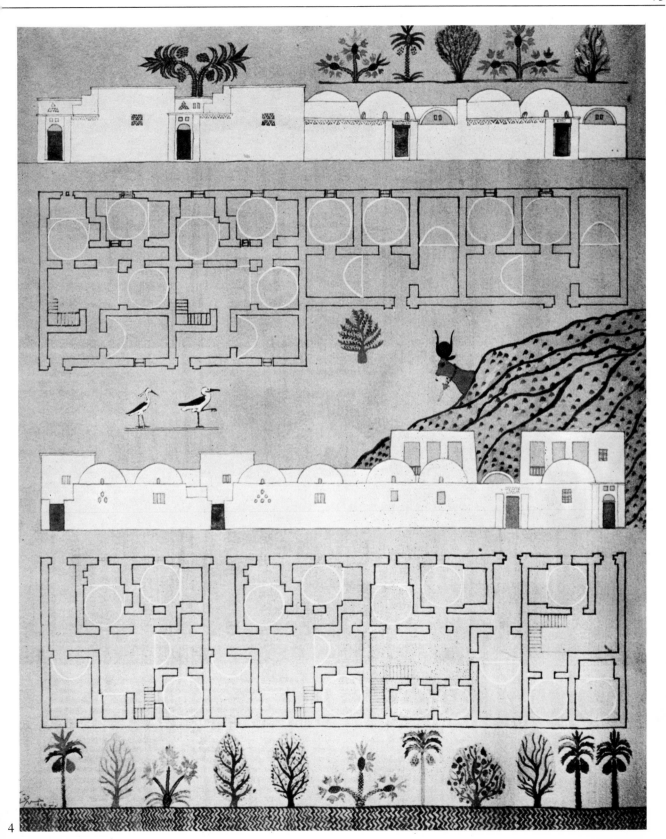

4

## Architects and Architects' Houses

**1–3** Interior and exterior of a villa built in 1980 near Luxor in Egypt, by the French architect Olivier Sednaoui in collaboration with David Sims. This vast home is one of the first built for middle-class needs by an architect in the Third World. (Photos by Christine Bastin, 1981)

**4, 5** (*Above*) The Egyptian architect Hassan Fathy and (*below*) the Nubian master-builder in mud, Aladdin Moustapha.

**6** Model of an anthropomorphic house of unbaked earth to be built in tiers, conceived by the French architect Guy Rottier in 1975. The contoured mound is here seen from above. (Photo by Guy Rottier)

**7, 8** One of the bedrooms of the house built in 1977 by the French architect Roger Katan and the Colombian architect Margareta Pacheco, at Sélingué in Mali. Strong prejudices persist against building in unbaked earth which is wrongly seen as 'poor' and 'primitive'. Its supporters are often suspected of rejecting 'progress' and industrial techniques. In order to prove the opposite, these architects built their own home out of unbaked earth. (Portraits by Anne Moreau, 1980 and photo of the house by Sergio Domian, 1981)

I

3

## An Agricultural Cooperative
## by Hassan Fathy in Egypt

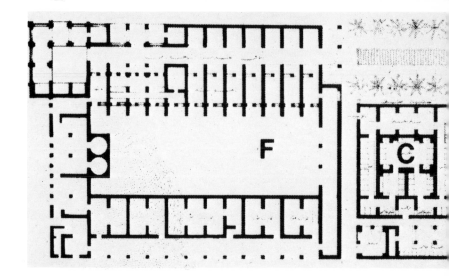

**1–5** Agricultural cooperative built by the architect Hassan Fathy, at Baris in the Kharga oasis in Egypt. The modernized 'Nubian vault' is used for roofing (*see* p. 60, ill. **6d**), as is the principle of through-ventilation to ensure permanent and effective air-conditioning. (Photo by Jacques Evrard and Christine Bastin, 1980)

(*Below*)  Plan of the entire complex of Baris, and two cross-sections of the agricultural cooperative indicating the principle of natural ventilation. (Drawings by Hassan Fathy)

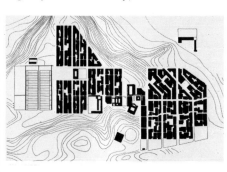

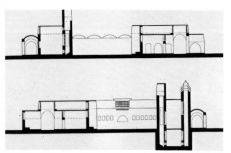

## La Luz: Suburb of Albuquerque, New Mexico

2

**1–9** Current enthusiasm in the USA for a revival of unbaked-earth building has led to the construction not only of individual houses but also of schemes on an urban scale: in 1975 the American architect Antoine Predock (**2**) built the residential district of 'La Luz' containing 100 luxury homes (**3**, **4** and **5**). This magnificent project proves that large modern schemes for urban housing can be constructed in unbaked earth, that developers can guarantee the safety of these structures, and that they can use the material interestingly. It also proves that earth architecture is adaptable to all types of cultural expression, from the traditional to the most up-to-date. This scheme is judged a milestone in contemporary American culture, and is listed in the *National Register of Historic Places*. The walls, made of adobe bricks with a protective covering, are encased around the top in a concrete sheath which is continuous with the slabs of the roof. (Plan and air-photo by Antoine Predock; portrait of the architect and photos of the house by Jacques Evrard and Christine Bastin, 1981)

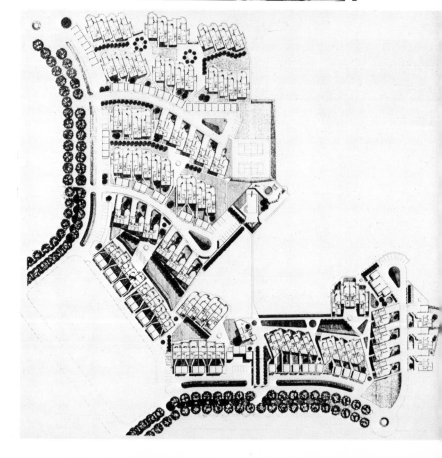

## Solar Houses of Unbaked Earth in the USA

**1, 5** 'Harrison Residence' was built by the American architect Adrien Dewint at Santa Fe, New Mexico, in 1979. It makes use of passive solar energy ('passive solar adobe'). (Photos by Jacques Evrard and Christine Bastin, 1981)

**2** A semi-subterranean house designed to employ passive solar energy, built in 1980 in unbaked earth by architects Georgina and John Mac Gowan near Santa Fe, New Mexico. (Photo by Christine Bastin, 1981)

**3, 4** Adobe house on split levels that make the best possible use of passive solar energy. 'Karen Terry House' was built in 1975 at Santa Fe, New Mexico, by David Wright, one of the American pioneers of bioclimatic architecture. (Photo by Jacques Evrard, 1981)

**6, 7** Exterior and interior of the 'Balcomb Residence' built in 1978 at Santa Fe, New Mexico, by William Lumpkins. He was one of the first people in America, long before the energy crisis, to try to revitalize regional traditions of earth architecture. (Photos by Jacques Evrard, 1981)

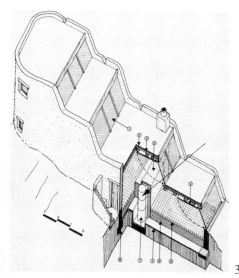

3

6

# New Agricultural Villages in China and Algeria

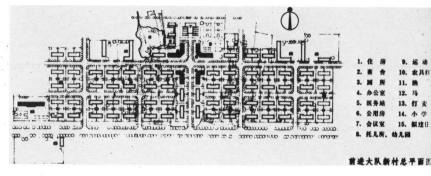

**1** Plan of an agricultural village built in unbaked earth *c.* 1960 in a Chinese commune, as part of regional development activities based on the concept that 'we must rely on our own resources'. (Plan provided by André Stevens)

**2–5** Agricultural village of Maadher built in blocks of stabilized earth by two architects, the El Miniawy brothers, near M'Sila in Algeria in 1980. (Photos by Jacques Evrard, 1981)

# Villas and a Community Center in the USA

**6, 7** Exterior and interior of a luxury villa built in raw earth in 1980 by the architect William Lumpkins near Taos, New Mexico. (Photos by Jacques Evrard and Christine Bastin, 1981)

**8** Interior of a bioclimatic villa built in unbaked earth in 1979 by the architect Robert Peters, near Santa Fe, New Mexico. (Photo provided by Robert Peters)

**9** Meditation room in the 'Lama Foundation', built in unbaked earth *c.* 1973 in New Mexico. (Photo by Jacques Evrard, 1981)

## Housing Projects and New Towns

**1** Residential avenue at Fort Davis, Texas, built in the 19th century. The houses are entirely of unbaked earth, except for the pillars of the verandahs. (Photo by Robin K. Laughlin, 1980)

**2, 3** Public buildings in the center of Adrar, the new town built *c.* 1930 in the Algerian Sahara. (Photos by Karl-Heinz Striedter, 1971)

**4** Low-budget housing estate, built in 1882 in unbaked earth at Saint-Simeon de Bressieux near Grenoble in France. The architect of these buildings remains unidentified, but they constitute one of the best examples of the influence of the 18th-century pioneer theorist François Cointeraux (*see* p. 149, ill. 6). This prototype of industrial architecture in *pisé* was 'rediscovered' in 1981, and the CRATerre group from Grenoble – who study and evaluate this mode of construction – has proposed that it be declared a historic monument and protected as part of the regional heritage. (Photo by Patrice Doat and Hugo Houben, 1981)

**5** Mosque built *c.* 1930 in the center of the new town of Adrar in the Algerian Sahara. (Photo by Karl-Heinz Striedter, 1971)

(*Below*) Plan of the new town of Timimoun in Algeria.

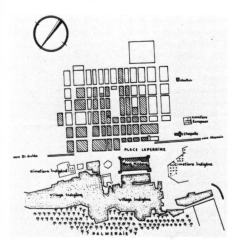

4

5

# Chronological Bibliography: from 1772 to 1981

## A selection of references

**1772** GOIFFON, M. *L'Art du maçon piseur* (Le Jai, Paris)

**1777** DIDEROT, D. 'Pisay, pisey, pisé' (*Encyclopaedia*, sup. vol. 4, p. 384, Paris)

**1790** COINTERAUX, F. *Ecole d'architecture rurale ou leçons par lesquelles on apprendra soi-même à bâtir solidement les maisons de plusieurs étages avec la terre seule . . .* (Chez l'auteur à Paris)

**1793** COINTERAUX, F. *Schule der Landbaukunst* (Hildberghaussen, Germany)

**1802** BARBER, WILLIAM *Farm Buildings; or rural economy . . . a description of the mode of building in pisé* (For the author, London)

**1806** JOHNSON, S. W. *Rural Economy; containing a treatise on pisé building as recommended by the Board of Agriculture in Great Britain* (J. Riley and Co., New York)

**1818** GILLY, D. *Handbuch der Land-Baukunst* (Friedrich Bieweg, Braunschweig)

**1821** COINTERAUX, F. *Pisé, or the Art of building Strong and Durable Walls, to the height of several stories with nothing but earth . . .*, translated from the French [*see* **1790**] by Henry Holland (American Farmer, Baltimore)

**1825** SACHS, S. *Unleitung zur Erd-Bau-Kunst und Pisé-Bau* (Berlin)

**1837** FORD, RICHARD 'On Cob Walls' (*The Quarterly Review*, lviii, 529, England)

**1839** GILMAN, E. *The Economical Builder: a treatise on tapia and pisé walls* (J. Gideon Jr, Washington DC)

**1840** CONRADI, ERNST *Ueber den Pisé-Bau* (Kretschmar, Chemnitz, Germany)

**1841** WIMPF, W. J. *Der Pisé-Bau* (Heilbronn, Germany)

**1865** ENGEL, FRIEDRICH *Kalk-Sand-Pisé-Bau* (Wiegandt, Hampel und Parey, Berlin)

**1875** VIOLLET LE DUC, E. E. *Histoire de l'habitation humaine* (Paris)

**1899** *The Possibilities of Adobe* (*The Denver Times*, 14 May, Denver)

**1910** ADAM, J. W. *Adobe as a Building Material for the Plains* (Colorado Agricultural and Mechanical College, Fort Collins, Colorado)

**1919** KUNTZEL, C. *Lehmbauten* (Berlin)

**1919** WILLIAMS-ELLIS, CLOUGH *Building in Cob, Pisé and Stabilized Earth* (Country Life, England. New edition revised and enlarged by John and Elizabeth Eastwick-Fields, 1947)

**1920** RITGEN, O. V. *Volkswohnung-en und Lehmbau* (Berlin)

**1921** 'Germany Returns to Adobe Building' (*Engineering News Record*, 12 May, USA)

**1922** MANSON, J. LEASK and others *Building in Cob and Pisé de Terre* (Special Report no. 5, Building Research Board, Department of Scientific and Industrial Research, England)

**1923** 'Adobe Bricks made for Modern Building' (*Popular Mechanics*, February, USA)

**1924** ELLINGTON, KARL and INEZ *Modern Pisé Building: House building with compressed or rammed earth (pisé de terre): a revelation for the farmer and settler* (London)

**1926** ELLINGTON, KARL J. 'More Mud Houses' (*Scientific American*, March, USA)

**1928** WILLIAMS, MARY O'BRIEN 'Just a Mud House but it won a National Prize' (*Sunset*, October, USA)

**1937** LEE, A. B. *Houses of Earth* (Washington DC)

**1937** BETTS, M. C. and MILLER, T. A. H. *Rammed Earth Walls for Buildings* (Farmers Bulletin no. 1500, US Department of Agriculture)

**1937** 'Mud House Comes Back: New weatherproofing process revives ancient building art' (*Popular Science*, June, USA)

**1939** 'Cotton and Mud Go Into Houses: Government's effort to use native materials in low cost rural housing' (*Business Week*, 28 October, USA)

**1941** LE CORBUSIER *Les Murondins* (Paris)

**1945** GLENN, H. E. *Rammed Earth Building Construction* (Clemson State College, South Carolina)

**1946** FAUTH, WILHELM *Der praktische lehmbau* (Limes Verlag, Wiesbaden)

**1946** ALLER, PAUL and DAVIS *Build your own Adobe* (Stanford University Press, Stanford, California)

**1947** 'How Germans build Mud Homes' (*Popular Science*, November, USA)

**1947** KIENLIEN 'Le Béton de terre' (*Revue du génie militaire*, May, Paris)

**1947** HOLSCHER, WILHELM *Lehmbauordnung* (Verlag von Wilhelm Ernst und Sohn, Berlin)

**1950** CLOUGH, RICHARD H. *A Qualitative Comparison of Rammed Earth and Sundried Brick* (University of New Mexico Press, Albuquerque, New Mexico)

**1952** MIDDLETON, M. F. *Earth Wall Construction* (revised by L. M. Schneider and reprinted in 1981 by Australian Government Publishing Service, Canberra, Australia)

**953** MIDDLETON, M. F. *Build your House of Earth* (revised by Bob Young and reprinted in 1979 by Compendium Ltd., Victoria, Australia)

**956** *Earth for Homes* (American Agency for International Development, Washington DC) Reprinted 1974

**958** *Habitations en béton de terre stabilisée* (United Nations, New York)

**959** RISOM, SVEN *Nordiske Ler-Jords-huse* (Rosenkilde og Bagger, Copenhagen)

**961** LEBEUF, JEAN PAUL *L'Habitation des Fali, montagnards du Cameroun Central: technologie, sociologie, mythologie et symbolisme* (Hachette, Paris)

**962** JACQUES-MEUNIÉ, D. *Architectures et habitats du Dadès: Maroc présaharien* (Klincksieck, Paris)

**964** *Le Béton de terre stabilisée: son emploi dans la construction* (United Nations, New York)

**970** FATHY, HASSAN *Construire avec le peuple; histoire d'un village d'Egypte: Gourna* (Editions Sinbad, Paris)

**970** *A Study of the Feasibility of Mechanized Adobe Production* (Center for Environmental Research and Development, University of New Mexico, Albuquerque, New Mexico)

**971** BOUDREAU, EUGÈNE *Making the Adobe Brick* (Fifth Street Press, Berkeley, California)

**972** DETHIER, JEAN and BAUER, GÉRARD 'La Terre et le roseau ou la réhabilitation et l'amélioration des techniques traditionelles de construction au Maroc' (*Architecture d'Aujourd'hui*, no. 160, March, Paris)

**973** FATHY, HASSAN *Architecture for the Poor* (University of Chicago Press, Chicago and London)

**975** STEDMAN, MYRTHE and WILFRED *Adobe Architecture* (Sunstone Press, Santa Fe, New Mexico)

**976** GRAY, VIRGINIA and MACRAE, ALAN *Mud, Space and Spirit: Handmade Adobes* (Capa Press, Santa Barbara, California)

**1976** ARCHER, J. and G. *Dirt Cheap* (Compendium, Victoria, Australia)

**1976** BUNTING, BAINBRIDGE *Early Architecture in New Mexico* (University of New Mexico Press, Albuquerque, New Mexico)

**1976** KERN, KEN *The Owner Built Home* (Schribner's Sons, New York)

**1977** LEWIS, MILES *Victorian Primitive* (Greenhouse Publications, Carlton, Victoria, Australia)

**1977** RAINER, ROLAND *Anonymes Bauen in Iran/Traditional Building in Iran* (Akademische Verlag, Graz, Austria)

**1978** McHENRY, P. *Adobe Build-it-yourself* (University of Arizona Press, Tucson, Arizona)

**1978** KAHANE, JEFF *Local Materials: A Self Builder's Manual* (Publications Distribution Cooperative, London)

**1978** BARDOU, PATRICK and ARZOUMANIAN, VAROUJAM *Archi (tectures) de terre* (Editions Parenthèses, Paris) Published in Spanish by Gili, Barcelona

**1979** CRATERRE: DOAT, PATRICE, HOUBEN, HUGO and others *Construire en terre* (Editions Alternatives et Parallèles, Paris)

**1979** HOPSON, REX C. *Adobe: A Comprehensive Bibliography* (The Lightning Tree, Santa Fe, New Mexico)

**1980** MILLER, DAVID and LYDIA *Manual for Building a Rammed Earth Wall* (Miller, Greely, Colorado)

**1980** LUNT, M. G. *Stabilised Soil Blocks for Building* (Overseas Building Notes no. 184, February, Garston, Watford, England)

**1980** KHALILI, N. *Geltafan Earth: A Revolution in the Traditional Architecture of Iran* (Museum of Contemporary Arts, Teheran)

**1980** BERNARDOT, MARIE-JO 'Le Retour de la maison en terre' (*Le Monde*, 18 May, Paris)

**1981** DETHIER, JEAN 'Perché le architetture di terra nel 1981?' (*Interni*, Special Issue: 'Architetture di Terra', October, Milan)

**1981** 'La Terre: matériau d'avenir' (*Revue de l'habitat Social*, Special Issue containing 16 articles, no. 66, September, Paris)

**1981** 'Pourquoi les architectures en terre en 1981?' (Collection of articles in *Techniques et Architecture*, October, Paris)

**1981** LUMPKINS, WILLIAM *Casa del Sol; Thirty Proven Plans. Your Guide to Passive Solar House Design* (Santa Fe Publishing Company, Santa Fe, New Mexico)

**1981** KAPLAN, MICHAEL *Earth Building in Israel* (Jacob Blaustein Institute for Desert Research, Ben Gurion University of the Negev, Israel)

**1981** AGARWAL, ANIL *Mud, Mud: The potential of earth-based materials for Third World housing* (Earthscan, London). Also published in French and Spanish by Earthscan

**1981** EATON, RUTH 'Mud: An Examination of Earth Architecture' (*The Architectural Review*, pp. 222–30, October, London)

**1981** CRATERRE *Des architectures de terre/On Architecture in Unbaked Earth*; a bilingual booklet with 24 colour slides (Centre Georges Pompidou, CCI, Paris)

**1981** DETHIER, JEAN *Architecture in Unbaked Earth or the Future of Time-Honoured Traditions for industrialised and developing societies*; a portfolio of 90 photographic panels with trilingual texts – English, French, Spanish (Centre Georges Pompidou, CCI, Paris)

**1981** EMMOTT, DOUGLAS 'A Mud Revival' (*Development Forum*, no. 87, September, United Nations, Geneva)

## INDEX OF ARCHITECTS AND ENGINEERS: ILLUSTRATED WORKS
*Numerals refer to page numbers*

## INDEX OF COUNTRIES APPEARING IN ILLUSTRATIONS
*Numerals refer to page numbers*

We would like to express our most profound thanks to all those photographers, architects and engineers whose work is published here.